Poems for
Mothers

© 2009 by The Foundry Creative Media Company Limited

This 2009 edition published by Barnes & Noble, Inc., by arrangement with Star Fire

Star Fire is part of The Foundry Creative Media Company Limited

STAR FIRE BOOKS
Crabtree Hall, Crabtree Lane
Fulham, London SW6 6TY
United Kingdom
www.star-fire.co.uk

Publisher and Creative Director: Nick Wells
Project Editor and Selection: Victoria Lyle
Designer: Theresa Maynard

Barnes & Noble, Inc.
122 Fifith Avenue
New York, NY 10011

ISBN 978-1-4351-1054-0

Printed in Thailand

3 5 7 9 10 8 6 4 2

Every effort has been made to contact copyright holders. We apologize in advance for any omissions and would be pleased to insert the appropriate acknowledgement in subsequent editions of this publication.

While every endeavour has been made to ensure the accuracy of the reproduction on the images in this book, we would be grateful to receive any comments or suggestions for inclusion in future reprints.

Thanks to: Catherine Emslie, Victoria Garrard, Chris Herbert, Rebecca Kidd and Sara Robson

Poems for
Mothers

Victoria Lyle

STAR FIRE BOOKS

Contents

The bond between a mother and a child is an ancient, powerful and universal one. It is no wonder that many poets have been inspired to write about the arrival of a new life, particularly a child that, as Julia Neely Finch puts it, is 'flesh of my flesh', 'heart of my heart'. Equally, considering the multitude of roles a mother performs throughout a child's life, there are of course numerous poets that have expressed their gratitude and reciprocal love for their mothers in poetry. This collection brings these poems together to celebrate this special relationship.

The first chapter, 'A Mother's Love', celebrates the powerful feelings mothers have for their children. These are awakened even before birth, as demonstrated by Anna Laetitia Aikin Barbauld in 'To a Little Invisible Being'. The astonishment and awe felt when this child arrives and the wonder experienced on looking at their child's ear or cheek is beautifully evoked. This love remains undiminished and unconditional throughout their life and takes many forms, as later chapters explore.

The second chapter is a collection of 'Games, Rhymes and Lullabies' that mothers play, say or sing with their child. These poems demonstrate the mutual enjoyment that can be had together. Many of these games are timeless, such as 'Peek-A-Boo' by Ella Wheeler Wilcox, and all are simple, imaginative and fun. Settling a child down to sleep is an intimate and special time. These lullabies and cradle songs invoke a magical dreamy world, whilst also assuring children of their security.

'A Helping and Guiding Hand' examines the ways in which mothers demonstrate their love for their children in practical ways; by washing and dressing them, caring for them when they are sick, comforting them when they are upset and by teaching them right and wrong.

Perhaps one of the hardest parts of motherhood is watching their baby grow up and become independent, all the time worrying about what the future will hold for their beloved. The poems in 'Hopes and Fears' explore these issues. They celebrate landmarks, such as a child's first tooth or step, whilst also addressing a mother's concerns about the trials it is inevitable their children will face. Although some dream of fame and fortune for their child, the simple hope of all mothers is for health and happiness.

Finally, but perhaps most importantly, is 'Ode to Mothers', a selection of poems that thank mothers for everything they have done and continue to do, and expresses the child's love for their mother.

Poetry attempts to express fundamental truths about human nature and emotion in a beautiful and eloquent way. There is perhaps no more human a relationship than that between a mother and a child. Organised by theme, this collection looks at the myriad facets of this important bond.

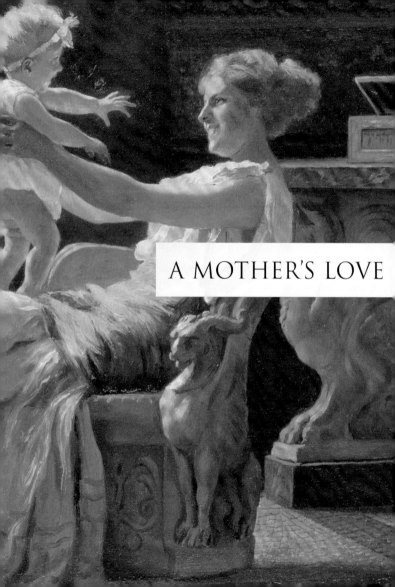

A MOTHER'S LOVE

To a Little Invisible Being
Who is Expected Soon to Become Visible

Germ of new life, whose powers expanding slow
For many a moon their full perfection wait,
Haste, precious pledge of happy love, to go
Auspicious borne through life's mysterious gate.
What powers lie folded in thy curious frame,
Senses from objects locked, and mind from thought!
How little canst thou guess thy lofty claim
To grasp at all the worlds the Almighty wrought!
And see, the genial season's warmth to share,
Fresh younglings shoot, and opening roses glow!
Swarms of new life exulting fill the air,
Haste, infant bud of being, haste to blow!
For thee the nurse prepares her lulling songs,
The eager matrons count the lingering day;
But far the most thy anxious parent longs
On thy soft cheek a mother's kiss to lay.
She only asks to lay her burden down,
That her glad arms that burden may resume;

And nature's sharpest pangs her wishes crown,
That free thee living from thy living tomb.
She longs to fold to her maternal breast
Part of herself, yet to herself unknown;
To see and to salute the stranger guest,
Fed with her life through many a tedious moon.
Come, reap thy rich inheritance of love!
Bask in the fondness of a Mother's eye!
Nor wit nor eloquence her heart shall move
Like the first accents of thy feeble cry.
Haste, little captive, burst thy prison doors!
Launch on the living world, and spring to light!
Nature for thee displays her various stores,
Opens her thousand inlets of delight.
If charmed verse or muttered prayers had power,
With favouring spells to speed thee on thy way,
Anxious I'd bid my beads each passing hour,
Till thy wished smile thy mother's pangs o'erpay.

Anna Laetitia Aikin Barbauld (1743–1825)

Infant Joy

'I have no name;
I am but two days old.'
What shall I call thee?
'I happy am,
Joy is my name.'
Sweet joy befall thee!

Pretty joy!
Sweet joy, but two days old.
Sweet Joy I call thee:
Thou dost smile,
I sing the while;
Sweet joy befall thee!

William Blake (1757–1827)

Extract from Frost at Midnight

Dear Babe, that sleepest cradled by my side,
Whose gentle breathings, heard in this deep calm,
Fill up the interspersèd vacancies
And momentary pauses of the thought!
My babe so beautiful! It thrills my heart
With tender gladness, thus to look at thee....

Samuel Taylor Coleridge (1772–1834)

To Ianthe

I love thee, Baby! For thine own sweet sake;
Those azure eyes, that faintly dimpled cheek,
Thy tender frame, so eloquently weak,
Love in the sternest heart of hate might wake;
But more when o'er thy fitful slumber bending
Thy mother folds thee to her wakeful heart,
Whilst love and pity, in her glances blending,
All that thy passive eyes can feel impart:
More, when some feeble lineaments of her,
Who bore thy weight beneath her spotless bosom,
As with deep love I read thy face, recur,
More dear art thou, O fair and fragile blossom;
Dearest when most thy tender traits express
The image of thy mother's loveliness.

Percy Bysshe Shelley (1792–1822)

Extract from The Dream

Sweet is the image of the brooding dove!
Holy as Heaven a mother's tender love!
The love of many prayers and many tears,
Which changes not with dim declining years,
The only love which on this teeming earth
Asks no return from Passion's wayward birth;
The only love that, with a touch divine,
Displaces from the heart's most secret shrine
The idol SELF.

Caroline Elizabeth Sarah Norton (1808–77)

The Mother's Heart

I

When first thou camest, gentle, shy, and fond,
My eldest-born, first hope, and dearest treasure,
My heart received thee with a joy beyond
All that it yet had felt of earthly pleasure;
Nor thought that any love again might be
So deep and strong as that I felt for thee.

II

Faithful and true, with sense beyond thy years,
And natural piety that lean'd to Heaven;
Wrung by a harsh word suddenly to tears,
Yet patient of rebuke when justly given –
Obedient, easy to be reconciled,
And meekly-cheerful – such wert thou, my child!

III

Not willing to be left; still by my side
Haunting my walks, while summer-day was dying; –
Nor leaving in thy turn; but pleased to glide
Thro' the dark room where I was sadly lying,
Or by the couch of pain, a sitter meek,
Watch the dim eye, and kiss the feverish cheek.

IV

O boy! Of such as thou are oftenest made
Earth's fragile idols; like a tender flower,
No strength in all thy freshness, prone to fade,

And bending weakly to the thunder-shower,
Still, round the loved, thy heart found force to bind,
And clung, like woodbine shaken in the wind!

V

Then THOU, my merry love; bold in thy glee,
Under the bough, or by the firelight dancing,
With thy sweet temper, and thy spirit free,
Didst come, as restless as a bird's wing glancing,
Full of a wild and irrepressible mirth,
Like a young sunbeam to the gladden'd earth!

VI

Thine was the shout! The song! The burst of joy!
Which sweet from childhood's rosy lip resoundeth;
Thine was the eager spirit nought could cloy,
And the glad heart from which all grief reboundeth;
And many a mirthful jest and mock reply,
Lurk'd in the laughter of thy dark-blue eye!

VII

And thine was many an art to win and bless,
The cold and stern to joy and fondness warming;
The coaxing smile; the frequent soft caress;
The earnest tearful prayer all wrath disarming!
Again my heart a new affection found,
But thought that lore with thee had reach'd its bound.

VIII
At length THOU camest; thou, the last and least;
Nick-named 'The Emperor' by thy laughing brothers,
Because a haughty spirit swell'd thy breast,
And thou didst seek to rule and sway the others;
Mingling with every playful infant wile
A mimic majesty that made us smile:

IX
And oh! Most like a regal child wert thou!
An eye of resolute and successful scheming!
Fair shoulders, curling lip, and dauntless brow –
Fit for the world's strife, not for Poet's dreaming:
And proud the lifting of thy stately head,
And the firm bearing of thy conscious tread.

X
Different from both! Yet each succeeding claim,
I, that all other love had been forswearing,
Forthwith admitted, equal and the same;
Nor injured either, by this love's comparing,
Nor stole a fraction for the newer call –
But in the Mother's heart, found room for ALL!

Caroline Elizabeth Sarah Norton (1808–77)

Lines Written October 23, 1836
A Few Hours After the Birth of My First Child

Beautiful babe, I gaze upon thy face
That bears no trace of earth: thy silk-soft cheek
Gladdens me even to tears, and thy full eyes
Blue as the midnight heaven; what thoughts are they
That flit across thy being, now faint smiles
Awakening, now thy tiny fairy fingers
Weaving in restless play? Above thee bends
An eye that drinks sweet pleasure from thine own,
A face of meaning wonderful and deep,
A form in every member full of love.
Once thou wert hidden in her painful side,
A boon unknown, a mystery and a fear;
Strange pangs she bore for thee; but He, whose name
Is everlasting Love, hath healed her pain,
And paid her suffering hours with living joy.

Thou gentle creature, now thine eyes are hid
In soft Elysian sleep: a holy calm
Hath settled on thee, and thy little hands
Are folded on thy breast. Thus could I look
For ever on thee, babe, with yearning heart
And strange unwonted pleasure. And thou too,
Sweet mother, hast been dallying with sleep
Till thou hast yielded; and I sit alone,
Alone, as if by Providence divine,
To watch in spirit, and in peaceful verse
To speak my thankfulness and purest joy.

Some, with the gift of song, have prophesied
High duties for their offspring: and the words,
Fresh from the parent heart, have wrought a charm
Upon their childhood and their growing youth;
And life hath taken colour from their love.
And thou, my little Alice, now so frail,
So new to the new world, in after-years
Shalt feel the wondrous tide of poesy
Rise in thy swelling breast; the happy earth,
And every living thing; spring with its leaves,
And summer clad in flowers, and autumn flush
With ripe abundance, and the winter frost,
Shall lay the deep foundations of thy soul
In peace and purity. Thence thou shalt love
The tale of strange adventure; watch the dance
Of moonlit fairies on the crisping grass,
And nurse thy little joys unchecked and free
With rhymes antique and laughter-loving sports,
With wanton gambols in the sunny air,
And in the freshening bath of rocky streams.

But God hath knowledge of the years between:
Fair be thy lot, my first and early born;
The pledge and solace of our life-long love.

Henry Alford (1810–71)

Sonnet 69
To Alice in England. Written in Frankfort.

Child of our love, thou sleepest softly now
In our dear home perchance, with thine own smile
Resting upon thy rosy lips, the while
Thy little arm is folded on thy brow,
And thou art dreaming of the summer flowers
Shown thee this sunny morn. Blest be thy sleep!
Good angels round thy bed their watches keep
In holy station through the silent hours.
Thus we commit thee to the wakeful care
Of Him whose mercy gave thee; thus secure
We leave thee in the confidence of prayer,
Of thy best welfare and his blessing sure;
Near, though to these our earthly eyes unseen;
With us, though half the ocean rolls between.

Henry Alford (1810–71)

Mother and Babe

I see the sleeping babe, nestling the breast of its mother;
The sleeping mother and babe – hush'd, I study them
    long and long.

Walt Whitman (1819–92)

Baby May

Cheeks as soft as July peaches,
Lips whose dewy scarlet teaches
Poppies paleness – round large eyes
Ever great with new surprise,
Minutes fill'd with shadeless gladness,
Minutes just as brimm'd with sadness,
Happy smiles and wailing cries,
Crows and laughs and tearful eyes,
Lights and shadows swifter born
Than on wind-swept Autumn corn,
Ever some new tiny notion
Making every limb all motion –
Catching up of legs and arms,
Throwings back and small alarms,
Clutching fingers – straightening jerks,
Twining feet whose each toe works,
Kickings up and straining risings,
Mother's ever new surprisings,
Hands all wants and looks all wonder
At all things the heavens under,
Tiny scorns of smil'd reprovings
That have more of love than lovings,
Mischiefs done with such a winning
Archness, that we prize such sinning,
Breakings dire of plates and glasses,
Graspings small at all that passes,
Pullings off of all that's able
To be caught from tray or table;

Silences – small meditations,
Deep as thoughts of cares for nations,
Breaking into wisest speeches,
In a tongue that nothing teaches,
All the thoughts of whose possessing
Must be wooed to light by guessing;
Slumbers – such sweet angel-seemings,
That we'd ever have such dreamings,
Till from sleep we see thee breaking,
And we'd always have thee waking;
Wealth for which we know no measure,
Pleasure high above all pleasure,
Gladness brimming over gladness,
Joy in care – delight in sadness,
Loveliness beyond completeness,
Sweetness distancing all sweetness,
Beauty all that beauty may be,
That's May Bennett, that's my baby.

William Cox Bennett (1820–95)

Extract from A Mother Showing the Portrait of Her Child

Living child or pictured cherub,
    Ne'er o'ermatched its baby grace;
And the mother, moving nearer,
    Looked it calmly in the face;
Then with slight and quiet gesture,
    And with lips that scarcely smiled,
Said – 'A Portrait of my daughter
    When she was a child.'

Easy thought was hers to fathom,
    Nothing hard her glance to read,
For it seemed to say, 'No praises
    For this little child I need:
If you see, I see far better,
    And I will not feign to care
For a stranger's prompt assurance
    That the face is fair.'

Jean Ingelow (1820–97)

Baby

Where did you come from, baby dear?
Out of the everywhere into here.

Where did you get those eyes so blue?
Out of the sky as I came through.

What makes the light in them sparkle and spin?
Some of the starry twinkles left in.

Where did you get that little tear?
I found it waiting when I got here.

What makes your forehead so smooth and high?
A soft hand stroked it as I went by.

What makes your cheek like a warm white rose?
I saw something better than any one knows.

Whence that three-cornered smile of bliss?
Three angels gave me at once a kiss.

Where did you get this pearly ear?
God spoke, and it came out to hear.

Where did you get those arms and hands?
Love made itself into bonds and bands.

Feet, whence did you come, you darling things?
From the same box as the cherubs' wings.

How did they all just come to be you?
God thought about me, and so I grew.

But how did you come to us, you dear?
God thought about you, and so I am here.

George MacDonald (1824–1905)

Thank God for Little Children

Thank God for little children,
Bright flowers by earth's wayside,
The dancing, joyous lifeboats
Upon life's stormy tide.

Thank God for little children;
When our skies are cold and gray,
They come as sunshine to our hearts,
And charm our cares away.

I almost think the angels,
Who tend life's garden fair,
Drop down the sweet wild blossoms
That bloom around us here.

It seems a breath of heaven
Round many a cradle lies,
And every little baby
Brings a message from the skies.

Dear mothers, guard these jewels.
As sacred offerings meet,
A wealth of household treasures
To lay at Jesus' feet.

Frances Ellen Watkins (1825–1911)

Mother to Babe

I
Fleck of sky you are,
Dropped through branches dark,
O my little one, mine!
Promise of the star,
Outpour of the lark;
Beam and song divine.

II
See this precious gift,
Steeping in new birth
All my being, for sign
Earth to heaven can lift,
Heaven descend on earth,
Both in one be mine!

III
Life in light you glass
When you peep and coo,
You, my little one, mine!
Brooklet chirps to grass,
Daisy looks in dew
Up to dear sunshine.

George Meredith (1828–1909)

To a Young Mother on the Birth of Her First Born Child

Young mother! Proudly throbs thine heart, and well may it rejoice,
Well may'st thou raise to Heaven above in grateful prayer thy voice:
A gift hath been bestowed on thee, a gift of priceless worth,
Far dearer to thy woman's heart than all the wealth of earth.

What store of deep and holy joy is opened to thy thought –
Glad, sunny dreams of future days, with bliss and rapture fraught;
Of hopes as varied, yet as bright, as beams of April sun,
And plans and wishes centred all within thy darling one!

While others seek in changing scenes earth's happiness to gain,
In fashion's halls to win a joy as dazzling as 'tis vain –
A bliss more holy far is thine, far sweeter and more deep,
To watch beside thine infant's couch and bend above his sleep.

What joy for thee to ling'ring gaze within those cloudless eyes,
Turning upon thee with a glance of such sweet, strange surprise,
Or press a mother's loving kiss upon that fair, white brow,
Of all earth's weight of sin and care and pain unconscious now.

Then, as thy loved one's sleeping breath so softly fans thy cheek,
And gazing on that tiny form, so lovely, yet so weak,
A dream comes o'er thee of the time when nobly at thy side
Thy cherished son shall proudly stand, in manhood's lofty pride.

Yet a sad change steals slowly o'er thy tender, loving eye,
Thou twin'st him closer to thy heart, with fond and anxious sigh,
Feeling, however bright his course he too must suff'ring know,
Like all earth's children taste alike life's cup of care and woe.

But, oh! It lies within thy power to give to him a spell
To guard him in the darkest hour from sorrow safe and well;
Thou'lt find it in the narrow path the great and good have trod –
And thou thyself wilt teach it him – the knowledge of his God!

Rosanna Eleanor Leprohon (1829–79)

I Know a Baby, Such a Baby

I know a baby, such a baby,
Round blue eyes and cheeks of pink,
Such an elbow furrowed with dimples,
Such a wrist where creases sink.
'Cuddle and love me, cuddle and love me,'
Crows the mouth of coral pink:
Oh, the bald head, and, oh, the sweet lips,
And, oh, the sleepy eyes that wink!

Christina Georgina Rossetti (1830–94)

My Baby Has a Mottled Fist

My baby has a mottled fist,
My baby has a neck in creases;
My baby kisses and is kissed,
For he's the very thing for kisses.

Christina Georgina Rossetti (1830–94)

Love Me – I Love You

Love me – I love you,
Love me, my baby;
Sing it high, sing it low,
Sing it as may be.

Mother's arms under you;
Her eyes above you;
Sing it high, sing it low,
Love me – I love you.

Christina Georgina Rossetti (1830–94)

Our Little Ghost

Oft, in the silence of the night,
 When the lonely moon rides high,
When wintry winds are whistling,
 And we hear the owl's shrill cry,
In the quiet, dusky chamber,
 By the flickering firelight,
Rising up between two sleepers,
 Comes a spirit all in white.

A winsome little ghost it is,
 Rosy-cheeked, and bright of eye;
With yellow curls all breaking loose
 From the small cap pushed awry.
Up it climbs among the pillows,
 For the 'big dark' brings no dread,
And a baby's boundless fancy
 Makes a kingdom of a bed.

A fearless little ghost it is;
 Safe the night seems as the day;
The moon is but a gentle face,
 And the sighing winds are gay.
The solitude is full of friends,
 And the hour brings no regrets;
For, in this happy little soul,
 Shines a sun that never sets.

A merry little ghost it is,
  Dancing gayly by itself,
On the flowery counterpane,
  Like a tricksy household elf;
Nodding to the fitful shadows,
  As they flicker on the wall;
Talking to familiar pictures,
  Mimicking the owl's shrill call.

A thoughtful little ghost it is;
  And, when lonely gambols tire,
With chubby hands on chubby knees,
  It sits winking at the fire.
Fancies innocent and lovely
  Shine before those baby-eyes,
Endless fields of dandelions,
  Brooks, and birds, and butterflies.

A loving little ghost it is:
  When crept into its nest,
Its hand on father's shoulder laid,
  Its head on mother's breast,
It watches each familiar face,
  With a tranquil, trusting eye;
And, like a sleepy little bird,
  Sings its own soft lullaby.

Then those who feigned to sleep before,
  Lest baby play till dawn,
Wake and watch their folded flower,
  Little rose without a thorn.
And, in the silence of the night,
  The hearts that love it most
Pray tenderly above its sleep,
  'God bless our little ghost!'

Louisa May Alcott (1832–88)

Extract from Man's Pillow

A baby lying on his mother's breast
Draws life from that sweet fount;
He takes his rest
And heaves deep sighs;
With brooding eyes
Of soft content
She shelters him within that fragrant nest,
And scarce refrains from crushing him
With tender violence,
His rosebud mouth, each rosy limb
Excite such joy intense;
Rocked on that gentle billow,
She sings into his ear
A song that angels stoop to hear.
Blest child and mother doubly blest!
Such his first pillow.

Irving Browne (1834–99)

Mother-Song
From 'Prince Lucifer' 2

White little hands!
Pink little feet!
Dimpled all over,
Sweet, sweet, sweet!
What dost thou wail for?
The unknown? The unseen?
The ills that are coming,
The joys that have been?

Cling to me closer,
Closer and closer,
Till the pain that is purer
Hath banish'd the grosser.
Drain, drain at the stream, love,
Thy hunger is freeing,
That was born in a dream, love,
Along with thy being!

Little fingers that feel
For their home on my breast,
Little lips that appeal
For their nurture, their rest!
Why, why dost thou weep, dear?
Nay, stifle thy cries,
Till the dew of thy sleep, dear,
Lies soft on thine eyes.

Alfred Austin (1835–1913)

Babyhood

I
A baby shines as bright
If winter or if May be
On eyes that keep in sight
  A baby.

Though dark the skies or grey be,
It fills our eyes with light,
If midnight or midday be.

Love hails it, day and night,
The sweetest thing that may be
Yet cannot praise aright
  A baby.

II
All heaven, in every baby born,
All absolute of earthly leaven,
Reveals itself, though man may scorn
  All heaven.

Yet man might feel all sin forgiven,
All grief appeased, all pain outworn,
By this one revelation given.

Soul, now forget thy burdens borne:
Heart, be thy joys now seven times seven:
Love shows in light more bright than morn
  All heaven.

III
What likeness may define, and stray not
    From truth's exactest way,
A baby's beauty? Love can say not
    What likeness may.

The Mayflower loveliest held in May
    Of all that shine and stay not
Laughs not in rosier disarray.

Sleek satin, swansdown, buds that play not
    As yet with winds that play,
Would fain be matched with this, and may not:
    What likeness may?

IV
Rose, round whose bed
Dawn's cloudlets close,
Earth's brightest-bred
    Rose!

No song, love knows,
May praise the head
Your curtain shows.

Ere sleep has fled,
The whole child glows
One sweet live red
    Rose.

Algernon Charles Swinburne (1837–1909)

Mine

Her eyes are bright as sparkling stars,
And as the violet blue;
In them celestial beauty lies,
The soul-light flashing through.
No painter, how e'er great his skill,
Can imitate her hair;
Naught save a sunset sea of gold
Had ever shade so rare.
The lilies with pale roses blend,
And melt upon her cheek –
Her carmine lips disclose seed pearls,
When e'er they ope to speak!
Her tiny ear, like sea-side shell,
Pink ting'd, of perfect mould,
A moment gleams, then disappears,
Lost in the sea of gold.

Ah, should you see my birdie blithe,
In some lone sylvan dell,
You'd think she was a fairy child,
Made mortal by a spell.
Her voice! Ah, never tropoic bird
Could trill so sweet a glee;
Nor is the sad Aeolian harp
So full of melody.
My birdie speaks, no earthly strain
Could thus my spirit move,
For her sweet notes pierce through my heart,
And thrill the cords of love.
For this fair child, this fairy bright,
So nearly being divine,
To me is sunshine, hope and life –
For she is mine, all mine!

Mary Eliza Perine Tucker Lambert (1838–1938)

Motherhood

From out the front of being, undefiled,
    A life hath been upheaved with struggle and pain;
    Safe in her arms a mother holds again
That dearest miracle – a new-born child.
To moans of anguish terrible and wild,
    As shrieks the night-wind through an ill-shut pane,
    Pure heaven succeeds; and after fiery strain
Victorious woman smiles serenely mild.

Yea, shall she not rejoice, shall not her frame
    Thrill with a mystic rapture! At this birth,
The soul now kindled by her vital flame
    May it not prove a gift of priceless worth?
Some saviour of his kind whose starry fame
    Shall bring a brightness to the darkened earth.

Mathilde Blind (1841–96)

Baby Charley

He's fast asleep. See how, O Wife,
Night's finger on the lip of life
Bids whist the tongue, so prattle-rife,
   Of busy Baby Charley.

One arm stretched backward round his head,
Five little toes from out the bed
Just showing, like five rosebuds red,
   So slumbers Baby Charley.

Heaven-lights, I know, are beaming through
Those lucent eyelids, veined with blue,
That shut away from mortal view
   Large eyes of Baby Charley.

O sweet Sleep-Angel, throned now
On the round glory of his brow,
Wave thy wing and waft my vow
   Breathed over Baby Charley.

I vow that my heart, when death is nigh,
Shall never shiver with a sigh
For act of hand or tongue or eye
   That wronged my Baby Charley!

Sidney Lanier (1842–81)

Infant Eyes

Blood of my blood, bone of my bone,
Heart of my being's heart,
Strange visitant, yet very son;
All this, and more, thou art.

In thy soft lineaments I trace,
More winning daily grown,
The sweetness of thy mother's face
Transfiguring my own.

That grave but all untroubled gaze,
So rapt yet never dim,
Seems following o'er their starry ways
The wings of cherubim.

Two worlds man hardly may descry,
(For manhood clouds them o'er),
Commingled to mine inward eye
Are shadowed forth once more:

That lost world, whither man's regret
With fictive fancy turns;
That world to come, where brighter yet
The star of promise burns.

Time and his weary offspring Care
Fade in that gaze away;
One moment mystically fair
Lives on, one timeless day.

Ernest Myers (1844–1921)

Bear∂ and Baby

I say, as one who never feared
The wrath of a subscriber's bullet,
I pity him who has a beard
But has no little girl to pull it!

When wife and I have finished tea,
Our baby woos me with her prattle,
And, perching proudly on my knee,
She gives my petted whiskers battle.

With both her hands she tugs away,
While scolding at me kind o' spiteful;
You'll not believe me when I say
I find the torture quite delightful!

No other would presume, I ween,
To trifle with this hirsute wonder,
Else would I rise in vengeful mien
And rend his vandal frame asunder!

But when her baby fingers pull
This glossy, sleek, and silky treasure,
My cup of happiness is full –
I fairly glow with pride and pleasure!

And, sweeter still, through all the day
I seem to hear her winsome prattle,
I seem to feel her hands at play,
As though they gave me sportive battle.

Yes, heavenly music seems to steal
Where thought of her forever lingers,
And round my heart I always feel
The twining of her dimpled fingers!

Eugene Field (1850–95)

The Stork

Last night the Stork came stalking,
And, Stork, beneath your wing
Lay, lapped in dreamless slumber,
The tiniest little thing!
From Babyland, out yonder
Beside a silver sea,
You brought a priceless treasure
As gift to mine and me!

Last night my dear one listened –
And, wife, you knew the cry –
The dear old Stork has sought our home
A many times gone by!
And in your gentle bosom
I found the pretty thing
That from the realm out yonder
Our friend the Stork did bring.

Last night a babe awakened,
And, babe, how strange and new
Must seem the home and people
The Stork has brought you to;
And yet methinks you like them –
You neither stare nor weep,
But closer to my dear one
You cuddle, and you sleep!

Last night my heart grew fonder –
O happy heart of mine,
Sing of the inspirations
That round my pathway shine!
And sing your sweetest love-song
To this dear nestling wee
The Stork from 'Way-Out-Yonder
Hath brought to mine and me!

Eugene Field (1850–95)

Garden and Cradle

When our babe he goeth walking in his garden,
Around his tinkling feet the sunbeams play;
The posies they are good to him,
And bow them as they should to him,
As fareth he upon his kingly way;
And birdlings of the wood to him
Make music, gentle music, all the day,
When our babe he goeth walking in his garden.

When our babe he goeth swinging in his cradle,
Then the night it looketh ever sweetly down;
The little stars are kind to him,
The moon she hath a mind to him
And layeth on his head a golden crown;
And singeth then the wind to him
A song, the gentle song of Bethlem-town,
When our babe he goeth swinging in his cradle.

Eugene Field (1850–95)

The Unborn

Thou art my very own,
A part of me,
Bone of my bone
And flesh of my flesh.
And thou shalt be
Heart of my heart
And brain of brain –
In years that are to come to me and thee.

Before thou wast a being, made
Of spirit, as of flesh,
Thou didst sleep beneath the beats
Of my tumultuous heart, and drink,
With little aimless lips
And blind, unseeing eyes,
From every bursting vein
Replete with life's abundant flood.
Ay! Even of my very breath,
And from my blood
Thou didst imbibe the fresh
And glorious air, that holds the sweets
Of nature's sure and slow eclipse;
That ceaseless round of life and death
Which are the close entwinëd braid
Of all the seasons' subtle mesh
And endless chain.

In a soft and silken chamber set apart –
Here, just beneath my happy heart –
Thou didst lie at dreamy ease
While all my being paid
Its tribute unto thee.
What happy hours for thee and me!
As when a bird
Broods on its downy nest –
So would I sit
And watch the flit
Of idle shadows to and fro,
And brood upon my treasure hid
Within my willing flesh.
And when there stirred
A little limb, a tiny hand!
What rapturous thrills of ecstasy
Shook all my being to its inmost citadel!
Ah! None but she who has borne
A child beneath her breast may know
What wondrous thrill and subtle spell
Comes from this wondrous woven band
That binds a mother to her unborn child
Within her womb.
As in the earth –
That fragrant tomb
Of all that lives, or man or beast –
Soft blossoms bud and bloom and swell,
So didst thou from my body gain
Sweet sustenance and royal feast.

Then through the gates of priceless pain
Thou camest to me – fair, so fair,
And so complete
From rose-tipped feet
To silken hair!
And there beneath each pearly lid,
There glowed a jewel – passing rare!
It moves and breathes! It slakes its thirst
At my all-abundant breast!
Oh, moment born of life – of love!
Oh, rapture of all earth's high, high above!
Three lives in one –
By loving won!
My own, and thine,
Oh, bond divine!
Our little child! Our little child!

Julia Neely Finch (1850–1926)

Mother Song
From the Portuguese

Heavy my heart is, heavy to carry,
Full of soft foldings, of downy enwrapments –
And the outer fold of all is love,
And the next soft fold is love,
And the next, finer and softer, is love again;
And were they unwound before the eyes
More folds and more folds and more folds would unroll
Of love – always love,
And, quite at the last,
Deep in the nest, in the soft-packed nest,
One last fold, turned back, would disclose
You, little heart of my heart,
Laid there so warm, so soft, so soft,
Not knowing where you lie, nor how softly,
Nor why your nest is so soft,
Nor how your nest is so warm.
You, little heart of my heart,
You lie in my heart,
Warm, safe and soft as this body of yours,
This dear kissed body of yours that lies
Here in my arms and sucks the strength from my breast,
The strength you will break my heart with one of these days.

Edith Nesbit (1858–1924)

A Child's Kiss

Sweet is the maiden's kiss that tells
    The secret of her heart;
Holy the wife's – yet in them dwells
    Of earthliness a part;

While in a little child's warm kiss
    Is naught but heaven above,
So sweet it is, so pure it is,
    So full of faith and love.

'Tis like a violet in May
    That knows nor fear nor harm,
But cheers the wanderer on his way
    With its unconscious charm.

'Tis like a bird that carols free,
    And thinks not of reward,
But gives the world its melody
    Because it is a bard.

Arthur Weir (1864–1902)

A Mother's Jewels

The daughter of a hundred earls,
    No jewels has with mine to mate,
Though she may wear in flawless pearls
    The ransom of a mighty state.

Hers glitter for the world to see,
    But chill the breast where they recline:
My jewels warmly compass me,
    And all their brilliancy is mine.

My diamonds are my baby's eyes,
    His lips, sole rubies that I crave:
They came to me from Paradise,
    And not through labors of the slave.

My darling's arms my necklace make,
    'Tis Love that links his feeble hands,
And Death, alone, that chain can break,
    And rob me of those priceless bands.

Arthur Weir (1864–1902)

A Baby Running Barefoot

When the bare feet of the baby beat across the grass
The little white feet nod like white flowers in the wind,
They poise and run like ripples lapping across the water;
And the sight of their white play among the grass
Is like a little robin's song, winsome,
Or as two white butterflies settle in the cup of one flower
For a moment, then away with a flutter of wings.

I long for the baby to wander hither to me
Like a wind-shadow wandering over the water,
So that she can stand on my knee
With her little bare feet in my hands,
Cool like syringa buds,
Firm and silken like pink young peony flowers.

D.H. Lawrence (1885–1930)

GAMES, RHYMES
& LULLABIES

Extract from To an Infant Sleeping

Sweet baby boy! Thy soft cheek glows
An emblem of tile living rose:
Thy breath a zephyr seems to rise;
And placid are thy half-clos'd eyes;
And silent is thy snowy breast,
Which gently heaves in transient rest;
And dreaming is thy infant brain
Of pleasure, undisturb'd by pain.

Mary Elizabeth Robinson (1775–1818)

A Cradle Song

Sweet dreams form a shade,
O'er my lovely infants head.
Sweet dreams of pleasant streams,
By happy silent moony beams

Sweet sleep with soft down.
Weave thy brows an infant crown.
Sweet sleep Angel mild,
Hover o'er my happy child.

Sweet smiles in the night,
Hover over my delight.
Sweet smiles Mothers smiles,
All the livelong night beguiles.

Sweet moans, dovelike sighs,
Chase not slumber from thy eyes,
Sweet moans, sweeter smiles,
All the dovelike moans beguiles.

Sleep, sleep happy child,
All creation slept and smil'd.
Sleep sleep, happy sleep.
While o'er thee thy mother weep

Sweet babe in thy face,
Holy image I can trace.
Sweet babe once like thee.
Thy maker lay and wept for me

Wept for me for thee for all,
When he was an infant small.
Thou his image ever see.
Heavenly face that smiles on thee,

Smiles on thee on me on all,
Who became an infant small,
Infant smiles are His own smiles,
Heaven and earth to peace beguiles.

William Blake (1757–1827)

Cradle Song

Sleep, sleep, beauty bright,
Dreaming in the joys of night;
Sleep, sleep; in thy sleep
Little sorrows sit and weep.

Sweet babe, in thy face
Soft desires I can trace,
Secret joys and secret smiles,
Little pretty infant wiles.

As thy softest limbs I feel,
Smiles as of the morning steal
O'er thy cheek, and o'er thy breast
Where thy little heart doth rest.

O the cunning wiles that creep
In thy little heart asleep!
When thy little heart doth wake,
Then the dreadful night shall break.

William Blake (1757–1827)

Lullaby

Sleep, little baby, sleep, love, sleep!
    Evening is coming, and night is nigh;
Under the lattice the little birds cheep,
    All will be sleeping by and by.
       Sleep, little baby, sleep.

Sleep, little baby, sleep, love, sleep!
    Darkness is creeping along the sky;
Stars at the casement glimmer and peep,
    Slowly the moon comes sailing by.
       Sleep, little baby, sleep.

Sleep, little baby, sleep, love, sleep!
    Sleep till the dawning has dappled the sky;
Under the lattice the little birds cheep,
    All will be waking by and by.
       Sleep, little baby, sleep.

Horace Smith (1779–1849)

A Child

A child's a plaything for an hour;
    Its pretty tricks we try
For that or for a longer space –
    Then tire, and lay it by.

But I knew one that to itself
    All seasons could control;
That would have mock'd the sense of pain
    Out of a grievèd soul.

Thou straggler into loving arms,
    Young climber-up of knees,
When I forget thy thousand ways
    Then life and all shall cease.

Mary Lamb (1765–1847)

The Baby's Dance

Dance little baby, dance up high,
Never mind baby, mother is by;
Crow and caper, caper and crow,
There little baby, there you go;
Up to the ceiling, down to the ground,
Backwards and forwards, round and round;
Dance little baby, and mother shall sing,
With the merry coral, ding, ding, ding.

Ann Taylor (1782–1866)

A Child Asleep

How he sleepeth! Having drunken
    Weary childhood's mandragore,
From his pretty eyes have sunken
    Pleasures, to make room for more –
Sleeping near the withered nosegay, which he pulled the
    day before.

Nosegays! Leave them for the waking:
    Throw them earthward where they grew.
Dim are such, beside the breaking
    Amaranths he looks unto –
Folded eyes see brighter colours than the open ever do.

Heaven-flowers, rayed by shadows golden
    From the paths they sprang beneath,
Now perhaps divinely holden,
    Swing against him in a wreath –
We may think so from the quickening of his bloom and of
    his breath.

Vision unto vision calleth,
    While the young child dreameth on.
Fair, O dreamer, thee befalleth
    With the glory thou hast won!
Darker wert thou in the garden, yestermorn, by
    summer sun.

We should see the spirits ringing
   Round thee – were the clouds away.
'Tis the child-heart draws them, singing
   In the silent-seeming clay –
Singing! Stars that seem the mutest, go in music all the way.

As the moths around a taper,
   As the bees around a rose,
As the gnats around a vapour –
   So the Spirits group and close
Round about a holy childhood, as if drinking its repose.

Shapes of brightness overlean thee –
   Flash their diadems of youth
On the ringlets which half screen thee –
   While thou smilest... not in sooth
Thy smile... but the overfair one, dropt from some
   aethereal mouth.

Haply it is angels' duty,
   During slumber, shade by shade:
To fine down this childish beauty
   To the thing it must be made,
Ere the world shall bring it praises, or the tomb shall see
   it fade.

Softly, softly! Make no noises!
    Now he lieth dead and dumb –
Now he hears the angels' voices
    Folding silence in the room –
Now he muses deep the meaning of the Heaven-words as
    they come.

Speak not! He is consecrated –
    Breathe no breath across his eyes.
Lifted up and separated,
    On the hand of God he lies,
In a sweetness beyond touching – held in cloistral sanctities.

Could ye bless him – father, mother?
    Bless the dimple in his cheek?
Dare ye look at one another,
    And the benediction speak?
Would ye not break out in weeping, and confess yourselves
    too weak?

He is harmless – ye are sinful,
    Ye are troubled – he, at ease:
From his slumber, virtue winful
    Floweth outward with increase –
Dare not bless him! But be blessed by his peace – and
    go in peace.

Elizabeth Barrett Browning (1806–61)

Sweet and Low

Sweet and low, sweet and low,
Wind of the western sea,
Low, low, breathe and blow,
Wind of the western sea!
Over the rolling waters go,
Come from the dying moon, and blow,
Blow him again to me;
While my little one, while my pretty one, sleeps.

Sleep and rest, sleep and rest,
Father will come to thee soon;
Rest, rest, on mother's breast,
Father will come to thee soon;
Father will come to his babe in the best,
Silver sails all out of the west,
Under the silver moon:
Sleep, my little one, sleep, my pretty one, sleep.

Alfred Lord Tennyson (1809–92)

Extract from *Mother's Love*

A little in the doorway sitting,
The mother plied her busy knitting,
And her cheek so softly smil'd,
You might be sure, although her gaze
Was on the meshes of the lace,
Yet her thoughts were with her child.
But when the boy had heard her voice,
As o'er her work she did rejoice,
His became silent altogether,
And slily creeping by the wall,
He seiz'd a single plume, let fall
By some wild bird of longest feather;
And all a-tremble with his freak,
He touch'd her lightly on the cheek.

Oh, what a loveliness her eyes
Gather in that one moment's space,
While peeping round the post she spies
Her darling's laughing face!
Oh, mother's love is glorifying,
On the cheek like sunset lying;
In the eyes a moisten'd light,
Softer than the moon at night!

Thomas Burbidge (1816–92)

Extract from A Child's Treasures

Thou art home at last, my darling one,
  Flushed and tired with thy play,
From morning dawn until setting sun
  Hast thou been at sport away;
And thy steps are weary, hot thy brow,
  Yet thine eyes with joy are bright;
Ah! I read the riddle, show me now
  The treasures thou graspest tight.

A pretty pebble, a tiny shell,
  A feather by wild bird cast,
Gay flowers gathered in forest dell,
  Already withering fast,
Four speckled eggs in a soft brown nest,
  Thy last and thy greatest prize,
Such the things that fill with joy thy breast,
  With laughing light thine eyes.

Rosanna Eleanor Leprohon (1829–79)

Lullaby, Oh, Lullaby!

Lullaby, oh, lullaby!
Flowers are closed and lambs are sleeping;
Lullaby, oh, lullaby!
Stars are up, the moon is peeping;
Lullaby, oh, lullaby!
While the birds are silence keeping,
(Lullaby, oh, lullaby!)
Sleep, my baby, fall a-sleeping,
Lullaby, oh, lullaby!

Christina Georgina Rossetti (1830–94)

Holy Innocents

Sleep, little Baby, sleep,
The holy Angels love thee,
And guard thy bed, and keep
A blessed watch above thee.
No spirit can come near
Nor evil beast to harm thee:
Sleep, Sweet, devoid of fear
Where nothing need alarm thee.

The Love which doth not sleep,
The eternal arms around thee:
The shepherd of the sheep
In perfect love has found thee.
Sleep through the holy night,
Christ-kept from snare and sorrow,
Until thou wake to light
And love and warmth to-morrow.

Christina Georgina Rossetti (1830–94)

Mother Shake the Cherry-Tree

Mother shake the cherry-tree,
Susan catch a cherry;
Oh how funny that will be,
Let's be merry!
One for brother, one for sister,
Two for mother more,
Six for father, hot and tired,
Knocking at the door.

Christina Georgina Rossetti (1830–94)

Lullaby

Now the day is done,
Now the shepherd sun
Drives his white flocks from the sky;
Now the flowers rest
On their mother's breast,
Hushed by her low lullaby.

Now the glowworms glance,
Now the fireflies dance,
Under fern-boughs green and high;
And the western breeze
To the forest trees
Chants a tuneful lullaby.

Now 'mid shadows deep
Falls blessed sleep,
Like dew from the summer sky;
And the whole earth dreams,
In the moon's soft beams,
While night breathes a lullaby.

Now, birdlings, rest,
In your wind-rocked nest,
Unscared by the owl's shrill cry;
For with folded wings
Little Brier swings,
And singeth your lullaby.

Louisa May Alcott (1832–88)

The Shadow-Children

Little shadows, little shadows
Dancing on the chamber wall,
While I sit beside the hearthstone
Where the red flames rise and fall.
Caps and nightgowns, caps and nightgowns,
My three antic shadows wear;
And no sound they make in playing,
For the six small feet are bare.

Dancing gayly, dancing gayly,
To and fro all together,
Like a family of daisies
Blown about in windy weather;
Nimble fairies, nimble fairies,
Playing pranks in the warm glow,
While I sing the nursery ditties
Childish phantoms love and know.

Now what happens, now what happens?
One small shadow's tumbled down:
I can see it on the carpet
Softly rubbing its hurt crown.
No one whimpers, no one whimpers;
A brave-hearted sprite is this:
See! The others offer comfort
In a silent, shadowy kiss.

Hush! They're creeping; hush! They're creeping,
Up about my rocking-chair:
I can feel their loving fingers
Clasp my neck and touch my hair.
Little shadows, little shadows,
Take me captive, hold me tight,
As they climb and cling and whisper,
'Mother dear, good night! Good night!'

Louisa May Alcott (1852–88)

A Child's Fancy

'Hush, hush! Speak softly, Mother dear,
So that the daisies may not hear;
For when the stars begin to peep,
The pretty daisies go to sleep.

'See, Mother, round us on the lawn,
With soft white lashes closely drawn,
They've shut their eyes so golden-gay,
That looked up through the long, long day.

'But now they're tired of all the fun –
Of bees and birds, of wind and sun
Playing their game at hide-and-seek;
Then very softly let us speak.'

A myriad stars above the child
Looked down from heaven and sweetly smiled;
But not a star in all the skies
Beamed on him with his Mother's eyes.

She stroked his curly chestnut head,
And whispering very softly, said,
'I'd quite forgotten they might hear;
Thank you for that reminder, dear.'

Mathilde Blind (1841–96)

Cockie-Roosie-Ride

Pit the bairn on mammy's back,
   Ow'r her shuiders pit his feet;
Let me grup his wee fat legs,
   While his brithers laugh to see't.
Pit the stules anaith the chairs,
   Clear the hoose on ilka side;
Maunna fa' when mammy gies
   Her bairn a cockie-roosie-ride.

Is he ready? Here we gang,
   Jumpin' roun' the hoose wi' glee;
Stoppin' whiles afore the glass
   To let the lauchin' laddie see.
Losh me, hoo he gecks an' goos,
   An' shogs an' sweys frae side to side;
Is his heid, like some we ken,
   Turn'd wi' his cockie-roosie-ride.

No ae minute can I stan',
   Roun' the hoose we gang again,
While the rascal tries to mak'
   My mutch-strings ser' him for a rein.
Hoo he kicks an' tries to spur,
   An' thraws his face wi' very pride;
Gudesake! Has he min' o' men
   When at his cockie-roosie-ride.

What's the matter wi' him noo,
  That he's takin' sic a grup,
Signin' wi' the ither han'
  For Jock to han' him up his whup?
Wad the sorra really strike –
  Bairns are unco ill to guide –
Strike his mammy, on whase back
  He tak's his cockie-roosie-ride?

There, noo, juist as I had thocht,
  Struck the wa' press wi' his croon;
Whup an' strings are a' let gae,
  As I boo to set him doon.
What a greetin' bairn, an' yet
  Siccan knocks are ill to bide;
Bless him, he'll get waur, I doot,
  In life's cockie-roosie-ride.

Dinna greet, but cuddle doon
    Safe an' snug on mammy's knee;
Cuddle, an' she'll clap his heid,
    An' mak' it better in a wee.
See, he's sabbit into sleep,
    Thinkin' nae what may betide
When he turns a man, an' tak's
    Anither cockie-roosie-ride.

'This warl's naething mair
    But a ride to rich an' poor;
Up an' doon we ride oor day
    Gettin' mony a fa' an' cloor;
Then at last, when tir'd an' sair
    Wi' wan'erin' unco far an' wide,
Quately are we slippit doon
    Frae oor cockie-roosie-ride.

Alexander Anderson (1845–1909)

Through Sleepy-Land

Where do you go when you go to sleep,
   Little Boy! Little Boy! Where?
'Way – 'way in where's Little Bo-Peep,
And Little Boy Blue, and the Cows and Sheep
   A-wandering 'way in there, in there,
     A-wandering 'way in there!

And what do you see when lost in dreams,
　　Little Boy, 'way in there?
Firefly-glimmers and glowworm-gleams,
And silvery, low, slow-sliding streams,
　　And mermaids, smiling out – 'way in where
　　　　They're a-hiding – 'way in there!

Where do you go when the Fairies call,
　　Little Boy! Little Boy! Where?
Wade through the clews of the grasses tall,
Hearing the weir and the waterfall
　　And the Wee Folk – 'way in there, in there,
　　　　And the Kelpies – 'way in there!

And what do you do when you wake at dawn,
　　Little Boy! Little Boy! What?
Hug my Mommy and kiss her on
Her smiling eyelids, sweet and wan,
　　And tell her everything I've forgot
　　　　About, a-wandering 'way in there –
　　　　　　Through the blind-world 'way in there!

James Whitcomb Riley (1849–1916)

So, So, Rock-a-by So!

So, so, rock-a-by so!
Off to the garden where dreamikins grow;
And here is a kiss on your winkyblink eyes,
And here is a kiss on your dimpledown cheek
And here is a kiss for the treasure that lies
In the beautiful garden way up in the skies
Which you seek.
Now mind these three kisses wherever you go –
So, so, rock-a-by so!

There's one little fumfay who lives there, I know,
For he dances all night where the dreamikins grow;
I send him this kiss on your droopydrop eyes,
I send him this kiss on your rosyred cheek.
And here is a kiss for the dream that shall rise
When the fumfay shall dance in those far-away skies
Which you seek.
Be sure that you pay those three kisses you owe –
So, so, rock-a-by so!

And, by-low, as you rock-a-by go,
Don't forget mother who loveth you so!
And here is her kiss on your weepydeep eyes,
And here is her kiss on your peachypink cheek,
And here is her kiss for the dreamland that lies
Like a babe on the breast of those far-away skies
Which you seek –
The blinkywink garden where dreamikins grow –
So, so, rock-a-by so!

Eugene Field (1850–95)

Extract from A Lullaby

The stars are twinkling in the skies,
    The earth is lost in slumbers deep;
So hush, my sweet, and close thine eyes,
    And let me lull thy soul to sleep.
Compose thy dimpled hands to rest,
    And like a little birdling lie
Secure within thy cozy nest
Upon my loving mother breast,
    And slumber to my lullaby,
    So hushaby – O hushaby.

The moon is singing to a star
    The little song I sing to you;
The father sun has strayed afar,
    As baby's sire is straying too.
And so the loving mother moon
    Sings to the little star on high;
And as she sings, her gentle tune
Is borne to me, and thus I croon
    For thee, my sweet, that lullaby
    Of hushaby – O hushaby.

Eugene Field (1850–95)

The Way to Wonderland

Who knows the way to wonderland?
Oh, I know, Oh, I know!
Trotty-te-trot on mama's knee,
Then over the billows of sleepy sea,
Down through the straits of by-lo,
Oh, who but mama could understand
The ways that lead to wonderland.

Now we are off to wonderland,
You and I, you and I,
Into the harbor of happy dreams,
Oh how misty and fair it seems,
Rock, rock a-by;
Ah! No one but mama could understand
The way that leads to wonderland

Now we will anchor at wonderland.
Slow, slow, slow, slow.
The magic place where angels keep
Dreams for babies who fall to sleep,
Down we go, down we go,
Oh, who but mama could understand
How to anchor at wonderland.

Ella Wheeler Wilcox (1850–1919)

Five Little Toes in the Morning

This little toe is hungry,
This little toe is too,
This toe lies abed like a sleepy head,
And this toe cries 'Boo-hoo.'
This toe big and tall is the smartest of all
For he pops into stocking and shoe.

Ella Wheeler Wilcox (1850–1919)

Five Little Toes at Night

This little toe is tired,
This little toe needs rocking,
This little toe is sleepy you know,
But this little toe keeps talking,
This toe big and tall is the mischief of all,
For he made a great hole in his stocking.

Ella Wheeler Wilcox (1850–1919)

Peek-a-Boo

The cunningest thing that a baby can do
Is the very first time it plays peek-a-boo;

When it hides its pink little face in its hands,
And crows, and shows that it understands

What nurse, and mamma and papa, too,
Mean when they hide and cry, 'Peek-a-boo, peek-a-boo.'

Oh, what a wonderful thing it is,
When they find that baby can play like this;

And everyone listens, and thinks it true
That baby's gurgle means 'Peek-a-boo, peek-a-boo';

And over and over the changes are rung
On the marvelous infant who talks so young.

I wonder if any one ever knew
A baby that never played peek-a-boo, peek-a-boo.

'Tis old as the hills are. I believe
Cain was taught it by Mother Eve;

For Cain was an innocent baby, too,
And I am sure he played peek-a-boo, peek-a-boo.

And the whole world full of the children of men,
Have all of them played that game since then.

Kings and princes and beggars, too,
Everyone has played peek-a-boo, peek-a-boo.

Thief and robber and ruffian bold,
The crazy tramp and the drunkard old,

All have been babies who laughed and knew
How to hide, and play peek-a-boo, peek-a-boo.

Ella Wheeler Wilcox (1850–1919)

Questions

What do the roses do, mother,
Now that the summer's done?
They lie in the bed that is hung with red
And dream about the sun.

What do the lilies do, mother,
Now that there's no more June?
Each one lies down in her white nightgown
And dreams about the moon.

What can I dream of, mother,
With the moon and the sun away?
Of a rose unborn, of an untried thorn,
And a lily that lives a day!

Edith Nesbit (1858–1924)

All Through the Night

Sleep my child and peace attend thee,
All through the night
Guardian angels God will send thee,
All through the night.

Soft the drowsy hours are creeping
Hill and vale in slumber sleeping,
I my loving vigil keeping
All through the night.

While the moon her watch is keeping
All through the night
While the weary world is sleeping
All through the night.

O'er they spirit gently stealing
Visions of delight revealing
Breathes a pure and holy feeling
All through the night.

Love, to thee my thoughts are turning
All through the night
All for thee my heart is yearning,
All through the night.

Though sad fate our lives may sever
Parting will not last forever,
There's a hope that leaves me never,
All through the night.

Harold Edwin Boulton (1859–1935)

The Mother

Beneath the eaves there is another chair,
    And a bruised lily lies upon the walk,
    With the bright drops still clinging to its stalk.
Whose careless hand has dropped its treasure there?
And whose small form does that frail settee bear?
    Whose are that wooden shepherdess and flock,
    That noble coach with steeds that never balk?
And why the gate that tops the cottage-stair?

Ah! He has now a rival for her love,
    A chubby-cheeked, soft-fisted Don Juan,
Who rules with iron hand in velvet glove
    Mother and sire, as only Baby can.
See! There they romp, the mother and her boy,
He on her shoulders perched and wild with joy.

Arthur Weir (1864–1902)

A Secret

A little baby went to sleep
One night in his white bed,
And the moon came by to take a peep
At the little baby head.

A wind, as wandering winds will do,
Brought to the baby there
Sweet smells from some quaint flower that grew
Out on some hill somewhere.

And wind and flower and pale moonbeam
About the baby's bed
Stirred and woke the funniest dream
In the little sleepy head.

He thought he was all sorts of things
From a lion to a cat;
Sometimes he thought he flew on wings,
Or fell and fell, so that

When morning broke he was right glad
But much surprised to see
Himself a soft, pink little lad
Just like he used to be.

I would not give this story fame
If there were room to doubt it,
But when he learned to talk, he came
And told me all about it.

John Charles McNeill (1874–1907)

Lullaby

You are much too big to dandle,
And I will not leave the candle.
   Go to sleep.
You are growing naughty, rather,
And I'll have to speak to father.
   Go to sleep!
If you're good I shall not tell, then.
Oh, a story? Very well, then.
   Once upon a time, a king, named Crawley Creep,
Had a very lovely daughter…
You don't want a drink of water!
   Go to sleep! There! There! Go to sleep.

C.J. Dennis (1876–1938)

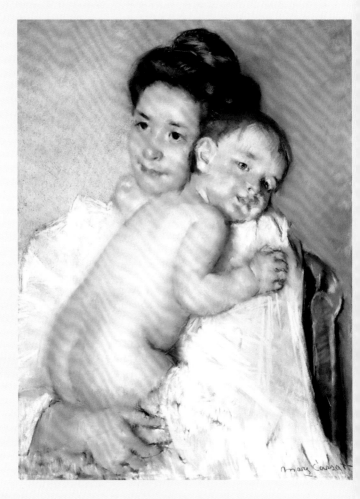

The Lonesome Child

The baby in the looking-glass
Is smiling through at me;
She has her teaspoon in her hand,
Her feeder on for tea.

And if I look behind her I
Can see the table spread;
I wonder if she has to eat
The nasty crusts of bread.

Her doll, like mine, is sitting close
Beside her special chair,
She has a pussy on her lap;
It must be my cup there.

Her picture-book is on the floor,
The cover's just the same;
And tidily upon the shelf
I see my Ninepin game.

O baby in the looking-glass,
Come through and play with me,
And if you will, I promise, dear,
To eat your crusts at tea.

Katherine Mansfield (1888–1923)

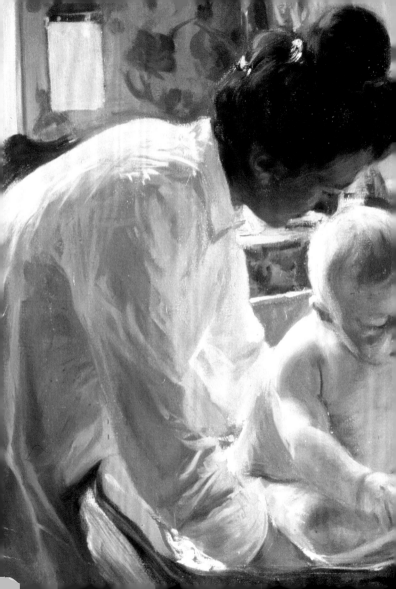

A HELPING &
GUIDING HAND

Poem 95

Unto his mother straight he weeping came,
and of his griefe complayned:
Who could not chose but laugh at his fond game,
though sad to see him pained.
Think now (quod she) my sonne how great the smart
of those whom thou dost wound:
Full many thou hast pricked to the hart,
that pitty neuer found:
Therefore henceforth some pitty take,
when thou doest spoyle of lovers make.

Edmund Spenser (1552–99)

Infant Sorrow

My mother groaned, my father wept,
Into the dangerous world I leapt;
Helpless, naked, piping loud,
Like a fiend hid in a cloud.

Struggling in my father's hands,
Striving against my swaddling bands,
Bound and weary, I thought best
To sulk upon my mother's breast.

William Blake (1757–1827)

If a Daughter You Have

If a daughter you have, she's the plague of your life,
No peace shall you know, tho' you've buried your wife,
At twenty she mocks at the duty you taught her,
O, what a plague is an obstinate daughter.
   Sighing and whining,
   Dying and pining,
O, what a plague is an obstinate daughter.

When scarce in their teens, they have wit to perplex us,
With letters and lovers for ever they vex us,
While each still rejects the fair suitor you've brought her,
O, what a plague is an obstinate daughter.
   Wrangling and jangling,
   Flouting and pouting,
O, what a plague is an obstinate daughter.

Richard Brinsley Sheridan (1751–1816)

Second Nursery Lesson (Admonitory)

Fat Tommy on the carpet lay,
And held with sprightly kit his play.
To her the twisted cord he flung,
At which with teeth and claws she sprung;
His worsted ball then past her roll'd,
Which soon within her clutching hold
She whirled, and checked, and tugged, and tore,
Then sent it rolling as before.
Tommy, his blue eyes glancing bright,
View'd all these antics with delight;
Then fondly stroked her tabby fur,
And smiled to see her wink and purr;
And then her ears began to touch,
Which she endured, but liked not much;
Then did her hinder parts assail,
And pinch'd and pull'd her by the tail.

On this her sudden anger rose,
She turn'd and growl'd, and scratched his nose.
Then Tommy roared like any bull
And said, his eyes with tears brim full,
'Mamma, beat kit.' 'And why?' quoth she.
'Beat naughty kit for scratching me,
And teach her not to scratch again.'
'No child, such teaching were in vain.
She can feel pain, but lacks the wit
To learn a lesson; but we'll hit
Upon a plan more plain and easy.
Tommy has sense to learn, so, please ye,
Let him be taught this simple lore,
To pull his play-mate's tail no more.'

Joanna Baillie (1762–1851)

About the Little Girl that Beat Her Sister

Go, go, my naughty girl, and kiss
    Your little sister dear;
I must not have such things as this,
    And noisy quarrels here.

What! Little children scratch and fight,
    That ought to be so mild;
Oh! Mary, it's a shocking sight
    To see an angry child.

I can't imagine, for my part,
    The reason for your folly;
She did not do you any hurt
    By playing with your dolly.

See, see, the little tears that run
    Fast from her watery eye:
Come, my sweet innocent, have done,
    'Twill do no good to cry.

Go, Mary, wipe her tears away,
    And make it up with kisses:
And never turn a pretty play
    To such a pet as this is.

Ann Taylor (1782–1866)

The Washing and Dressing

Ah! Why will my dear little girl be so cross,
    And cry, and look sulky, and pout?
To lose her sweet smile is a terrible loss,
    I can't even kiss her without.

You say you don't like to be wash'd and be dress'd,
    But would you not wish to be clean?
Come, drive that long sob from your dear little breast,
    This face is not fit to be seen.

If the water is cold, and the brush hurts your head,
    And the soap has got into your eye,
Will the water grow warmer for all that you've said?
    And what good will it do you to cry?

It is not to tease you and hurt you, my sweet,
    But only for kindness and care,
That I wash you, and dress you, and make you look neat,
    And comb out your tanglesome hair.

I don't mind the trouble, if you would not cry,
    But pay me for all with a kiss;
That's right, take the towel and wipe your wet eye,
    I thought you'd be good after this.

Ann Taylor (1782–1866)

Extract from Little Girls Must Not Fret

What is it that makes little Emily cry?
Come then, let mamma wipe the tear from her eye:
There, lay down your head on my bosom, that's right,
And now tell mamma what's the matter to-night.

Ann Taylor (1782–1866)

My Mother

Who sat and watched my infant head
When sleeping on my cradle bed,
And tears of sweet affection shed?
My Mother.

When pain and sickness made me cry,
Who gazed upon my heavy eye,
And wept for fear that I should die?
My Mother.

Who taught my infant lips to pray
And love God's holy book and day,
And walk in wisdom's pleasant way?
My Mother.

And can I ever cease to be
Affectionate and kind to thee,
Who wast so very kind to me,
My Mother?

Ah, no! The thought I cannot bear,
And if God please my life to spare
I hope I shall reward they care,
My Mother.

When thou art feeble, old and grey,
My healthy arm shall be thy stay,
And I will soothe thy pains away,
My Mother.

Ann Taylor (1782–1866)

Home, Sweet Home

Mid pleasures and palaces though we may roam,
Be it ever so humble, there's no place like home;
A charm from the sky seems to hallow us there,
Which, seek through the world, is ne'er met with elsewhere.
Home, home, sweet, sweet home!
There's no place like home, oh, there's no place like home!

An exile from home, splendor dazzles in vain;
Oh, give me my lowly thatched cottage again!
The birds singing gayly, that come at my call;
Give me them, and the peace of mind, dearer than all!
Home, home, sweet, sweet home!
There's no place like home, oh, there's no place like home!

I gaze on the moon as I tread the drear wild,
And feel that my mother now thinks of her child,
As she looks on that moon from our own cottage door
Thro' the woodbine, whose fragrance shall cheer me no more.
Home, home, sweet, sweet home!
There's no place like home, oh, there's no place like home!

How sweet 'tis to sit 'neath a fond father's smile,
And the caress of a mother to soothe and beguile!
Let others delight mid new pleasures to roam,
But give me, oh, give me, the pleasures of home.
Home, home, sweet, sweet home!
There's no place like home, oh, there's no place like home!

To thee I'll return, overburdened with care;
The heart's dearest solace will smile on me there;
No more from that cottage again will I roam;
Be it ever so humble, there's no place like home.
Home, home, sweet, sweet, home!
There's no place like home, oh, there's no place like home!

John Howard Payne (1791–1852)

A Faithful Mother's Love

Dear child! A faithful mother's love
   For thee will toil, and watch, and pray;
An angel hovering still above
   Thy couch by night, thy steps by day.

Oh think how oft thy lips have pressed
   Her breast! How oft thine arms have clung
Around her neck, while to her heart
   She clasped thee close, and sweetly sung!

When fever's burning flush suffused
   Thy cheek, and heaved thy panting chest,
Thou rest or refuge all refused
   Save mother's arms and mother's breast.

And she would sit with tangled hair,
   With haggard cheek and heavy eyes,
Tend all thy wants with loving care,
   And soothe thy pains and hush thy cries.

And she would whisper in thy ear,
   And press upon thy infant mind
The name, the love of Jesus dear,
   And God, thy Father good and kind.

The pouting lip, the pert reply,
    The sullen brow, the stubborn will,
Will dim with tears thy mother's eye,
    And her fond heart with anguish fill.

The smiling lip, the ready yes,
    The sunny brow of cheerful love;
What balm for mother's heart like this?
    What dearer blessing can she prove?

Is she a widow? Doubly dear
    Be she to thee; when griefs assail,
Kiss thou away each mournful tear
    That wanders down her cheek so pale.

A faithful God, the first, the best –
    The next a faithful mother's love;
Thou shalt, dear child, of these possessed,
    Be safe on earth, and blest above.

Janet Hamilton (1795–1873)

There Was a Place in Childhood

There was a place in childhood that
    I remember well,
And there a voice of sweetest tone,
    bright fairy tales did tell,
And gentle words, and fond embrace,
    were given with joy to me,
When I was in that happy place upon
    my mother's knee

Samuel Lover (1797–1868)

Extract from Aurora Leigh, Book 1

Women know
The way to rear up children (to be just),
They know a simple, merry, tender knack
Of tying sashes, fitting baby-shoes,
And stringing pretty words that make no sense,
And kissing full sense into empty words,
Which things are corals to cut life upon,
Although such trifles: children learn by such,
Love's holy earnest in a pretty play
And get not over-early solemnised,
But seeing, as in a rose-bush, Love's Divine
Which burns and hurts not, not a single bloom,
Become aware and unafraid of Love.
Such good do mothers.

Elizabeth Barrett Browning (1806–61)

Childhood

Childhood, sweet and sunny childhood,
　　With its careless, thoughtless air,
Like the verdant, tangled wildwood,
　　Wants the training hand of care.
See it springing all around us –
　　Glad to know, and quick to learn;
Asking questions that confound us;
　　Teaching lessons in its turn.
Who loves not its joyous revel,
　　Leaping lightly on the lawn,
Up the knoll, along the level,
　　Free and graceful as a fawn?
Let it revel; it is nature
　　Giving to the little dears
Strength of limb, and healthful features,
　　For the toil of coming years.
He who checks a child with terror,
　　Stops its play, and stills its song,
Not alone commits an error,
　　But a great and moral wrong.

Give it play, and never fear it –
　　Active life is no defect;
Never, never break its spirit –
　　Curb it only to direct.
Would you dam the flowing river,
　　Thinking it would cease to flow?
Onward it must go forever –
　　Better teach it where to go.
Childhood is a fountain welling,
　　Trace its channel in the sand,
And its currents, spreading, swelling,
　　Will revive the withered land.
Childhood is the vernal season;
　　Trim and train the tender shoot;
Love is to the coming reason,
　　As the blossom to the fruit.
Tender twigs are bent and folded –
　　Art to nature beauty lends;
Childhood easily is moulded;
　　Manhood breaks, but seldom bends.

David Bates (1809–70)

The Hand that Rocks the Cradle
Is the Hand that Rules the World

Blessings on the hand of women!
Angels guard its strength and grace,
In the palace, cottage, hovel,
Oh, no matter where the place;
Would that never storms assailed it,
Rainbows ever gently curled;
For the hand that rocks the cradle
Is the hand that rules the world.

Infancy's the tender fountain,
Power may with beauty flow,
Mother's first to guide the streamlets,
From them souls unresting grow –
Grow on for the good or evil,
Sunshine streamed or evil hurled;
For the hand that rocks the cradle
Is the hand that rules the world.

Woman, how divine your mission
Here upon our natal sod!
Keep, oh, keep the young heart open
Always to the breath of God!
All true trophies of the ages
Are from mother-love impearled;
For the hand that rocks the cradle
Is the hand that rules the world.

Blessings on the hand of women!
Fathers, sons, and daughters cry,
And the sacred song is mingled
With the worship in the sky –
Mingles where no tempest darkens,
Rainbows evermore are hurled;
For the hand that rocks the cradle
Is the hand that rules the world.

William Ross Wallace (1819–81)

Half-Waking

I thought it was the little bed
    I slept in long ago;
A straight white curtain at the head,
    And two smooth knobs below.
I thought I saw the nursery fire,
    And in a chair well-known
My mother sat, and did not tire
    With reading all alone.
If I should make the slightest sound
    To show that I'm awake,
She'd rise, and lap the blankets round,
    My pillow softly shake;
Kiss me, and turn my face to see
    The shadows on the wall,
And then sing Rousseau's Dream to me,
    Till fast asleep I fall.
But this is not my little bed;
    That time is far away;
With strangers now I live instead,
    From dreary day to day.

William Allingham (1824–89)

Extract from My Mother's Kiss

My mother's kiss, my mother's kiss,
I feel its impress now;
As in the bright and happy days
She pressed it on my brow.

You say it is a fancied thing
Within my memory fraught;
To me it has a sacred place –
The treasure house of thought.

Again, I feel her fingers glide
Amid my clustering hair;
I see the love-light in her eyes,
When all my life was fair.

Again, I hear her gentle voice
In warning or in love.
How precious was the faith that taught
My soul of things above.

Frances Ellen Watkins (1825–1911)

A Nursery Darling

A Mother's breast:
Safe refuge from her childish fears,
From childish troubles, childish tears,
Mists that enshroud her dawning years!
See how in sleep she seems to sing
A voiceless psalm – an offering
Raised, to the glory of her King
In Love: for Love is Rest.

A Darling's kiss:
Dearest of all the signs that fleet
From lips that lovingly repeat
Again, again, the message sweet!
Full to the brim with girlish glee,
A child, a very child is she,
Whose dream of heaven is still to be
At Home: for Home is Bliss.

Lewis Carroll (1832–98)

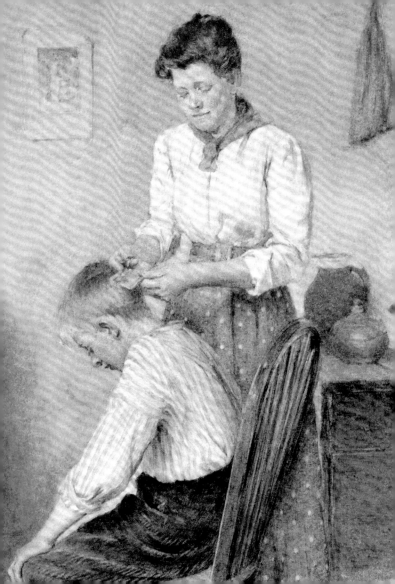

Extract from When Mother Combed My Hair

When Memory, with gentle hand,
Has led me to that foreign land
Of childhood days, I long to be
Again the boy on bended knee,
With head a-bow, and drowsy smile
Hid in a mother's lap the while,
With tender touch and kindly care,
She bends above and combs my hair.

Ere threats of Time, or ghosts of cares
Had paled it to the hue it wears,
Its tangled threads of amber light
Fell o'er a forehead, fair and white,
That only knew the light caress
Of loving hands, or sudden press
Of kisses that were sifted there
The times when mother combed my hair.

James Whitcomb Riley (1849–1916)

The Sick Child

Child

O mother, lay your hand on my brow!
O mother, mother, where am I now?
Why is the room so gaunt and great?
Why am I lying awake so late?

Mother

Fear not at all: the night is still.
Nothing is here that means you ill –
Nothing but lamps the whole town through,
And never a child awake but you.

Child

Mother, mother, speak low in my ear,
Some of the things are so great and near,
Some are so small and far away,
I have a fear that I cannot say.
What have I done, and what do I fear,
And why are you crying, mother dear?

Mother

Out in the city, sounds begin
Thank the kind God, the carts come in!
An hour or two more and God is so kind,
The day shall be blue in the windowblind,
Then shall my child go sweetly asleep,
And dream of the birds and the hills of sheep.

Robert Louis Stevenson (1850–94)

To Alison Cunningham
From Her Boy

For the long nights you lay awake
And watched for my unworthy sake:
For your most comfortable hand
That led me through the uneven land:
For all the story-books you read:
For all the pains you comforted:
For all you pitied, all you bore,
In sad and happy days of yore:
My second Mother, my first Wife,
The angel of my infant life –
From the sick child, now well and old,
Take, nurse, the little book you hold!

And grant it, Heaven, that all who read
May find as dear a nurse at need,
And every child who lists my rhyme,
In the bright, fireside, nursery clime,
May hear it in as kind a voice
As made my childish days rejoice!

Robert Louis Stevenson (1850–94)

The Cunnin' Little Thing

When baby wakes of mornings,
Then it's wake, ye people all!
For another day
Of song and play
Has come at our darling's call!
And, till she gets her dinner,
She makes the welkin ring,
And she won't keep still till she's had her fill –
The cunnin' little thing!

When baby goes a-walking,
Oh, how her paddies fly!
For that's the way
The babies say
To other folk 'by-by';
The trees bend down to kiss her,
And the birds in rapture sing,
As there she stands and waves her hands –
The cunnin' little thing!

When baby goes a-rocking
In her bed at close of day,
At hide-and-seek
On her dainty cheek
The dreams and the dimples play;
Then it's sleep in the tender kisses
The guardian angels bring
From the Far Above to my sweetest love –
You cunnin' little thing!

Eugene Field (1850–95)

Child and Mother

O mother-my-love, if you'll give me your hand,
    And go where I ask you to wander,
I will lead you away to a beautiful land –
    The Dreamland that's waiting out yonder.
We'll walk in a sweet posie-garden out there,
    Where moonlight and starlight are streaming,
And the flowers and the birds are filling the air
    With the fragrance and music of dreaming.

There'll be no little tired-out boy to undress,
    No questions or cares to perplex you,
There'll be no little bruises or bumps to caress,
    Nor patching of stockings to vex you;
For I'll rock you away on a silver-dew stream
    And sing you asleep when you're weary,
And no one shall know of our beautiful dream
    But you and your own little dearie.

And when I am tired I'll nestle my head
    In the bosom that's soothed me so often,
And the wide-awake stars shall sing, in my stead,
    A song which our dreaming shall soften.
So, Mother-my-Love, let me take your dear hand,
    And away through the starlight we'll wander,
Away through the mist to the beautiful land –
    The Dreamland that's waiting out yonder.

Eugene Field (1850–95)

Mother's Kisses

Baby was playing and down he fell, down he fell, down he fell,
Mama will kiss him and make him well,
Oh! What a miracle this is!
Baby was running and stubbed his toe, stubbed his toe,
    stubbed his toe,
If mama will kiss him the pain will go –
Magical mother's kisses.

Once an angel fair and calm,
Brewed a wondrous soothing balm
From the sweet immortal flowers,
Growing in the heavenly bowers,

Then the mothers of the earth,
All were called and told its worth.
'But anoint your lips with this,'
Said the angel, 'and your kiss

Shall have magic in its touch.'
Now 'tis plain to see why such
Soothing balm for bruise or wound
In a mother's kiss is found.

Baby was playing and down he fell, down he fell, down he fell,
Mama will kiss him, and make him well,
Oh! What a miracle this is.
Baby was running and stubbed his toe, stubbed his toe,
    stubbed his toe,
If mama kisses him, pain will go –
Magical mother's kisses.

Ella Wheeler Wilcox (1850–1919)

Extract from Fatherhood

A kiss, a word of thanks, away
    They're gone, and you forsaken learn
The blessedness of giving; they
    (So Nature bids) forget, nor turn
    To where you sit, and watch, and yearn.

And you (so Nature bids) would go
    Through fire and water for their sake;
Rise early, late take rest, to sow
    Their wealth, and lie all night awake
    If but their little finger ache.

Henry Charles Beeching (1859–1919)

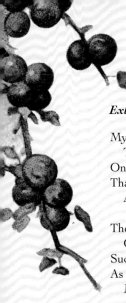

Extract from My Mother's Hand

My head is aching, and I wish
 That I could feel tonight
One well-remembered, tender touch
That used to comfort me so much,
 And put distress to flight.

There's not a soothing anodyne
 Or sedative I know,
Such potency can ever hold
As that which lovingly controlled
 My spirit long ago.

How oft my burning cheek as if
 By Zephyrus was fanned,
And nothing interdicted pain
Or seemed to make me well again
 So quick as mother's hand.

Hattie Howard (1860–1920)

Boys Will Be Boys

'Boys will be boys,' and boys have had their day;
   Boy-mischief and boy-carelessness and noise
Extenuated all, allowed, excused and smoothed away,
   Each duty missed, each damaging wild act,
   By this meek statement of unquestioned fact –
      Boys will be boys!

Now, 'women will be women.' Mark the change;
   Calm motherhood in place of boisterous youth;
No warfare now; to manage and arrange,
   To nurture with wise care, is woman's way,
   In peace and fruitful industry her sway,
      In love and truth.

Charlotte Perkins S. Gilman (1860–1935)

Scamp

Ain't it nice to have a mammy
W'en you kin' o' tiahed out
Wid a-playin' in de meddah,
An' a-runnin' roun' about
Till hit's made you mighty hongry,
An' yo' nose hit gits to know
What de smell means dat's a-comin'
F'om de open cabin do'?
She wash yo' face,
An' mek yo' place,
You's hongry as a tramp;
Den hit's eat you suppah right away,
You sta'vin' little scamp.

W'en you's full o' braid an' bacon,
An' dey ain't no mo' to eat,
An' de lasses dat's a-stickin'
On yo' face ta'se kin' o' sweet,
Don' you t'ink hit's kin' o' pleasin'
Fu' to have som'body neah
Dat'll wipe yo' han's an' kiss you
Fo' dey lif' you f'ore yo cheah?
To smile so sweet,
An' wash yo' feet,
An' leave 'em co'l an' damp;
Den hit's come let me undress you, now
You lazy little scamp.

Don' yo' eyes git awful heavy,
An' yo' lip git awful slack,
Ain't dey som'p'n' kin' o' weaknin'
In de backbone of yo' back?
Don' yo' knees feel kin' o' trimbly,
An' yo' head go bobbin' roun',
W'en you says yo' 'Now I lay me,'
An' is sno'in' on de 'down'?
She kiss yo' nose,
She kiss yo' toes,
An' den tu'n out de lamp,
Den hit's creep into yo' trunnel baid,
You sleepy little scamp.

Paul Laurence Dunbar (1872–1906)

'Urry

Now, Ma-til-der! Ain't cher dressed yet? I declare, the girl ain't up!
Last as ushul. Move yerself, you sleepy'-ead!
Are you goin' to lie there lazin',
W'ile I – Nell, put down that basin;
Go an' see if Bill has got the poddies fed;
Tell 'im not to move that clucky – ho, yer up, me L'-dy eh?
That's wot comes from gallivantin' lat ut night.
Why, the sun is nearly – see now,
Don't chu dare talk back at me now!
Set the table, Nell! Where's Nell? Put out that light!

Now then, 'urry, goodness, 'urry! Mary, tell the men to come.
Oh there, drat the girl! MA-TIL-DER! Where's the jam?
You fergot it? Well, uv all ther…
Mary! 'Ear me tell you call ther…
Lord! There's Baldy TANGLED IN THE BARB'-WIRE – SAM!
Now, then, take 'er steady, clumsy, or she'll cut herself –
    LEAVE OFF!
Do you want the cow to – There! I never did!
Well, you mighter took 'er steady.
Sit up, Dad, yer late already.
Did ju put the tea in, Mary? Where's the lid?

Oh, do 'urry! Where's them buckets? Nell, 'as Bill brought
     in the cows?
Where's that boy? Ain't finished eatin' yet, uv course;
Eat all day if 'e wus let to.
Mary, where'd yer father get to?
Gone! Wot! Call 'im back! DAD! Wot about that 'orse?
No, indeed, it ain't my business; you kin see the man yerself.
No, I won't! I'm sure I've quite enough to do.
If 'e calls ter-day about it,
'E kin either go without it,
Or elst walk acrost the paddick out to you.

Are the cows in, B-i-ll? Oh, there they are. Well, nearly time
     they – Nell,
Feed the calves, an' pack the – Yes, indeed ju will!
Get the sepy-rater ready.
Woa, there, Baldy – steady, steady.
Bail up. Stop-er! Hi, Matilder! MARY! BILL!
Well, uv all th'… Now you've done it.
Wait till Dad comes 'ome to-night;
When 'e sees the mess you've – Don't stand starin' there!
Go an' get the cart an' neddy;
An' the cream cans – are they ready?
Where's the… There! Fergot the fowls, I do declare!

Chuck! Chook! CHOOK! Why, there's that white un lost
    another chick to-day!
Nell, 'ow many did I count? Oh, stop that row!
Wot's 'e doin'? Oh, you daisy!
Do you mean to tell me, lazy,
Thet you 'aven't fed the pigs until jus' now?
Oh, do 'urry! There's the men ull soon be knockin' off fer lunch.
An' we 'aven't got the … Reach that bacon down.
Get the billies, Nell, an' – Mary,
Go an' fetch the … Wot? 'Ow dare 'e!
Bill, yer NOT to wear yer best 'at inter town!

'Ave you washed the things, Matilder? Oh, do 'urry, girl, yer late!
Seems to me you trouble more – TAKE CARE! – You dunce!
Now you've broke it! Well I never!
Ain't chu mighty smart an' clever;
Try'n to carry arf a dozen things at once.
No back answers now! You hussy! Don't chu dare talk back at me
Or I'll… Nelly, did ju give them eggs to Bill?
Wot? CHU NEVER? Well I … Mary,
Bring them dishes frum the dairy;
No, not them, the … Lord, the sun's be'ind the hill!

'Ave you cleaned the sepy-rater, Nell? Well, get along to bed.
No; you can't go 'crost to Thompson's place to-night;
You wus there las' Chusday – See, miss,
Don't chu toss your head at me, miss!
I won't 'ave it. Mary, 'urry with that light!
Now then, get yer Dad the paper. Set down, Dad – ju must
    be tired.
'Ere, Matilder, put that almanick away!
Where's them stockin's I wus darnin'?
Bill an' Mary, stop yer yarnin'!
Now then, Dad. Heigh-ho! Me fust sit down ter-day.

C.J. Dennis (1876–1938)

The Naughty Day

I've had a naughty day to-day.
    I scrunched a biscuit in my hair,
And dipped my feeder in the milk,
    And spread my rusk upon a chair.

When mother put me in my bath,
    I tossed the water all about,
And popped the soap upon my head,
    And threw the sponge and flannel out.

I wouldn't let her put my hand
    Inside the arm-hole of my vest;
I held the sleeve until she said
    I really never SHOULD be dressed.

And while she made the beds, I found
    Her tidy, and took out the hairs;
And then I got the water-can
    And tipped it headlong down the stairs.

I crawled along the kitchen floor,
    And got some coal out of the box,
And drew black pictures on the walls,
    And wiped my fingers on my socks.

Oh, this HAS been a naughty day!
    That's why they've put me off to bed.
'He CAN'T get into mischief there,
    Perhaps we'll have some peace,' they said.

They put the net across my cot,
    Or else downstairs again I'd creep.
But, see, I'll suck the counterpane
    To PULP before I go to sleep!

Fay Inchfawn (b. 1881)

A Little Boy's Dream

To and fro, to and fro
In my little boat I go
Sailing far across the sea
All alone, just little me.
And the sea is big and strong
And the journey very long.
To and fro, to and fro
In my little boat I go.

Sea and sky, sea and sky,
Quietly on the deck I lie,
Having just a little rest.
I have really done my best
In an awful pirate fight,
But we captured them all right.
Sea and sky, sea and sky,
Quietly on the deck I lie.

Far away, far away
From my home and from my play,
On a journey without end
Only with the sea for friend
And the fishes in the sea.
But they swim away from me
Far away, far away
From my home and from my play.

Then he cried 'O Mother dear.'
And he woke and sat upright,
They were in the rocking chair,
Mother's arms around him, tight.

Katherine Mansfield (1888–1923)

A Few Rules for Beginners

Babies must not eat the coal
And they must not make grimaces,
Nor in party dresses roll
And must never black their faces.

They must learn that pointing's rude,
They must sit quite still at table,
And must always eat the food
Put before them, if they're able.

If they fall, they must not cry,
Though it's known how painful this is;
No, there's always Mother by
Who will comfort them with kisses.

Katherine Mansfield (1888–1923)

The Black Monkey

My Babbles has a nasty knack
Of keeping monkeys on her back.
A great big black one comes and swings
Right on her sash or pinny strings.
It is a horrid thing and wild
And makes her such a naughty child.

She comes and stands beside my chair
With almost an offended air
And says: 'Oh, Father, why can't I?'
And stamps her foot and starts to cry –
I look at Mother in dismay…
What little girl is this, to-day?

She throws about her nicest toys
And makes a truly dreadful noise
Till Mother rises from her place
With quite a Sunday churchy face
And Babbles silently is led
Into the dark and her own bed.

Never a kiss or one Goodnight,
Never a glimpse of candle light.
Oh, how the monkey simply flies!
Oh, how poor Babbles calls and cries,
Runs from the room with might and main,
'Father dear, I am good again.'

When she is sitting on my knee
Snuggled quite close and kissing me,
Babbles and I, we think the same –
Why, that the monkey never came
Only a terrible dream maybe…
What did she have for evening tea?

Katherine Mansfield (1888–1923)

HOPES & FEARS

Going Into Breeches

Joy to Philip, he this day
Has his long coats cast away,
And (the childish season gone)
Puts the manly breeches on.
Officer on gay parade,
Red-coat in his first cockade,
Bridegroom in his wedding trim,
Birthday beau surpassing him,
Never did with conscious gait
Strut about in half the state,
Or the pride (yet free from sin)
Of my little Manikin:
Never was there pride, or bliss,
Half so rational as his.
Sashes, frocks, to those that need 'em –
Philip's limbs have got their freedom –
He can run, or he can ride,
And do twenty things beside,
Which his petticoats forbad: Is he not a happy lad?
Now he's under other banners,
He must leave his former manners;
Bid adieu to female games,
And forget their very names,
Puss-in-corners, hide-and-seek,
Sports for girls and punies weak!
Baste-the-bear he now may play at,
Leap-frog, foot-ball, sport away at,
Show his strength and skill at cricket,

Mark his distance, pitch his wicket,
Run about in winter's snow
Till his cheeks and fingers glow,
Climb a tree, or scale a wall,
Without any fear to fall.
If he get a hurt or bruise,
To complain he must refuse,
Though the anguish and the smart
Go unto his little heart,
He must have his courage ready,
Keep his voice and visage steady,
Brace his eye-balls stiff as drum,
That a tear may never come,
And his grief must only speak
From the colour in his cheek.
This and more he must endure,
Hero he in miniature!
This and more must now be done
Now the breeches are put on.

Charles Lamb (1775–1834)

The First Tooth

Sister

Through the house what busy joy,
Just because the infant boy
Has a tiny tooth to show.
I have got a double row,
All as white, and all as small;
Yet no one cares for mine at all.
He can say but half a word,
Yet that single sound's preferred
To all the words that I can say
In the longest summer day.
He cannot walk, yet if he put
With mimic motion out his foot,
As if he thought he were advancing,
It's prized more than my best dancing.

Brother

Sister, I know, you jesting are,
Yet O! of jealousy beware.
If the smallest seed should be
In your mind of jealousy,
It will spring, and it will shoot,
Till it bear the baneful fruit.
I remember you, my dear,
Young as is this infant here.
There was not a tooth of those
Your pretty even ivory rows,
But as anxiously was watched,
Till it burst its shell new hatched,
As if it a Phoenix were,
Or some other wonder rare.
So when you began to walk,
So when you began to talk,
As now, the same encomiums past.
'Tis not fitting this should last
Longer than our infant days;
A child is fed with milk and praise.

Charles Lamb (1775–1834)

The Mother

'And beats my heart again with joy!
　And dances now my spirit light!
The skiff that holds my darling boy
　This moment burst upon my sight!

'Not yet distinctly I perceive
　Amid the crew his well-known form,
But still his safety I believe,
　I know he has escap'd the storm.

'I feel as if my heart had wings,
　And tender from excess of bliss,
His form, which airy fancy brings,
　In fond emotion seem to kiss.

'Welcome the wild, imperfect rest,
　Which these bewilder'd spirits share!
Welcome this tumult of the breast,
　After the shudder of despair!

'My Robert he is brave and strong,
　He will these flowing tears reprove.
Alas! How little know the young,
　The tremor of a Mother's love.

'For we are weak from many a care,
　From many a sleepless, anxious hour,
When fear and hope the bosom tear,
　And ride the brain with fevering power.

'But lo! He cheerly waves his hand!
　I hear his voice! I see his face!
And eager now he springs to land,
　To meet a Mother's fond embrace!

'This failing heart! But joy to me,
　If heaven in pity is thy guard;
And of the pangs I feel for thee,
　Protection be the dear reward!'

Matilda Betham (1776–1852)

Extract from Maternal Hope

Lo! At the couch where infant beauty sleeps,
Her silent watch the mournful mother keeps:
She, while the lovely babe unconscious lies,
Smiles on her slumb'ring child with pensive eyes,
And weaves a song of melancholy joy:
'Sleep, image of thy father! Sleep, my boy!
No ling'ring hour of sorrow shall be thine,
No sigh that rends thy father's heart and mine.
Bright, as his manly sire, the son shall be,
In form and soul; but, ah! More blest than he!
Thy fame, thy worth, thy filial love, at last,
Shall soothe his aching heart for all the past;
With many a smile my solitude repay,
And chase the world's ungenerous scorn away.

Thomas Campbell (1777–1844)

The Child

See yon blithe child that dances in our sight!
Can gloomy shadows fall from one so bright?
   Fond mother, whence these fears?
While buoyantly he rushes o'er the lawn,
Dream not of clouds to stain his manhood's dawn,
   Nor dim that sight with tears.

No cloud he spies in brightly glowing hours,
But feels as if the newly vested bowers
   For him could never fade:
Too well we know that vernal pleasures fleet,
But having him, so gladsome, fair, and sweet,
   Our loss is overpaid.

Amid the balmiest flowers that earth can give
Some bitter drops distil, and all that live
   A mingled portion share;
But, while he learns these truths which we lament,
Such fortitude as ours will sure be sent,
   Such solace to his care.

Sara Coleridge (1802–50)

The Mother's Hope

Is there, when the winds are singing
In the happy summer time,
When the raptured air is ringing
With Earth's music heavenward springing

Forest chirp, and village chime,
Is there, of the sounds that float
Unsighingly, a single note
Half so sweet, and clear, and wild,
As the laughter of a child?

Listen! And be now delighted:
Morn hath touched her golden strings;
Earth and Sky their vows have plighted;
Life and Light are reunited

Amid countless carollings;
Yet, delicious as they are,
There's a sound that's sweeter far,
One that makes the heart rejoice
More than all, the human voice!

Organ finer, deeper, clearer,
Though it be a stranger's tone,
Than the winds or waters dearer,
More enchanting to the hearer,

For it answereth to his own.
But, of all its witching words,
Those are sweetest, bubbling wild
Through the laugher of a child.

Harmonies from time-touched towers,
Haunted strains from rivulets,
Hum of bees among the flowers,
Rustling leaves, and silver showers,

These, erelong, the ear forgets;
But in mine there is a sound
Ringing on the whole year round,
Heart-deep laughter that I heard
Ere my child could speak a word.

Ah! 'Twas heard by ear far purer,
Fondlier formed to catch the strain,
Ear of one whose love is surer,
Hers, the mother, the endurer

Of the deepest share of pain;
Here the deepest bliss to treasure
Memories of that cry of peasure;
Hers to hoard, a lifetime after,
Echoes of that infant laughter.

'Tis a mother's large affection
Hears with a mysterious sense,
Breathings that evade detection,
Whisper faint, and fine inflection,

Thrill in her with power intense.
Chidhood's honeyed words untaught
Hiveth she in loving thought,
Tones that never thence depart;
For she listens, with her heart.

Samuel Laman Blanchard (1803–45)

The Child Asleep
From The French

Sweet babe! True portrait of thy father's face,
Sleep on the bosom that thy lips have pressed!
Sleep, little one; and closely, gently place
Thy drowsy eyelid on thy mother's breast.

Upon that tender eye, my little friend,
Soft sleep shall come, that cometh not to me!
I watch to see thee, nourish thee, defend;
'Tis sweet to watch for thee, alone for thee!

His arms fall down; sleep sits upon his brow;
His eye is closed; he sleeps, nor dreams of harm.
Wore not his cheek the apple's ruddy glow,
Would you not say he slept on Death's cold arm?

Awake, my boy! I tremble with affright!
Awake, and chase this fatal thought! Unclose
Thine eye but for one moment on the light!
Even at the price of thine, give me repose!

Sweet error! He but slept! I breathe again;
Come, gentle dreams, the hour of sleep beguile!
Oh, when shall he, for whom I sigh in vain,
Beside me watch to see thy waking smile?

Henry Wadsworth Longfellow (1807–82)

On Seeing Anthony,
The Eldest Child of Lord and Lady Ashley

I

It was a fair and gentle child
Stood leaning by his mother's knee;
His noble brow was smooth and mild,
His eyes shone bright with frolic glee,
And he was stately, though so young;
As from a noble lineage sprung.

II

So, gazing on him, as we gaze,
Upon a bud, whose promise yet
Lies shut from all the glowing rays
Which afterwards illumine it:
I marvell'd what the fruit might be
When that fair plant became a tree.

III

Ah! Then, what dreams of proud success,
That lordly brow of beauty brought,
With all its infant stateliness,
And all its unripe power of thought!
What triumphs, boundless, unconfined,
Came crowding on my wand'ring mind!

IV

I gave that child, the voice might hold
A future senate in command;
Head clear and prompt, heart true and bold,
As quick to act as understand:
I dream'd the scholar's fame achieved,
The hero's wreath of laurel weaved!

V

But as I mused, a whisper came
Which like a friend's reproachful tone,
Whose gentleness can smite with shame
Far more than fiercest word or frown
Roused my vex'd conscience by its spell,
And thus the whisper'd warning fell:

VI

'Ah! Let the shrouded future be,
With all its weight of distant care!
Cloud not with dreams of vanity
That blue bright eye, and forehead fair!
Nor cast thy worldly hopes and fears
In shadow o'er his happy years!

VII
'Desire not, even in thy dreams,
To hasten those remoter hours
Which, bright although their promise seems,
Must strip his spring-time of its flowers!
What triumph, in the time to come,
Shall match these early days of home?

VIII
'This is the Eden of his life,
His little heart bounds glad and free:
Amid a world of toil and strife,
All independent smileth he!
Nor dreams by that sweet mother's side
Of dark Ambition's restless pride.

IX
'But, like a bird in winter, still
Fill'd with a sweet and natural joy,
Tho' frost lies bleak upon the hill,
And mists obscure the cold grey sky,
Which sings, tho' on a leafless bough,
He smiles, even at the gloomiest brow!'

X

Oh! Looking a child's fair face
Methinks should purify the heart;
As angel presences have grace
To bid the darker powers depart,
And glorify our grosser sense
With a reflected innocence!

XI

And seeing thee, thou lovely boy,
My soul, reproach'd, gave up its schemes
Of worldly triumph's heartless joy,
For purer and more sinless dreams,
And mingled in my farewell there
Something of blessing and of prayer.

Caroline Elizabeth Sarah Norton (1808–77)

Cradle Song

What does little birdie say
In her nest at peep of day?
Let me fly, says little birdie,
Mother, let me fly away.
Birdie, rest a little longer,
Till thy little wings are stronger.
So she rests a little longer,
Then she flies away.

What does little baby say,
In her bed at peep of day?
Baby says, like little birdie,
Let me rise and fly away.
Baby, sleep a little longer,
Till thy little limbs are stronger.
If she sleeps a little longer,
Baby too shall fly away.

Alfred Lord Tennyson (1809–92)

Extract from A Mother's Prayer

I knelt beside a little bed,
    The curtains drew away,
And, 'mid the soft, white folds beheld,
    Two rosy sleepers lay;
The one had seen three summers smile
    And lisped her evening prayer;
The other, only one year's shade
    Was on her flaxen hair.

No sense of duties ill performed
    Weighed on each heaving breast,
No weariness of work-day care
    Disturbed their tranquil rest;
The stars to them as yet were in
    The reach of baby hand,
Temptation, trial, grief, were words
    They could not understand.

Mary Gardiner Horsford (1824–55)

A Mother to Her Son on His Birthday

Thy natal day returns again,
Full fourteen suns have sped
Since first you woke to sin and pain,
Safe cradled in your bed.
'Twas then my dearest cares began,
My fondest hopes and fears;
To see your baby form a man,
To soothe you mid your tears.
From mid-day sun, from noisome damp,
To shade my darling boy;
To watch the waning flickering lamp,
When sickness did annoy.
To teach thy stubborn will to bend,
To lead thy mind aright;
To pray that God his power would lend,
And make thy virtues bright.
This since thy birth has been my care,
And now I would renew
Again my fondest latest pray'r
For every gift for you.
Implore of Him His grace to give,
His wings of love to spread;
To teach you early how to live,
Protect your infant head.
Thy mother's warmest accents hear,
My dearest blessing thou!
Reward her pangs, her cares, her fear;
Receive her dictates now!

Edward Henry Bickersteth (1825–1906)

Mother's Treasures

Two little children sit by my side,
I call them Lily and Daffodil;
I gaze on them with a mother's pride,
One is Edna, the other is Will.

Both have eyes of starry light,
And laughing lips o'er teeth of pearl.
I would not change for a diadem
My noble boy and darling girl.

To-night my heart o'erflows with joy;
I hold them as a sacred trust;
I fain would hide them in my heart,
Safe from tarnish of moth and rust.

What should I ask for my dear boy?
The richest gifts of wealth or fame?
What for my girl? A loving heart
And a fair and a spotless name?

What for my boy? That he should stand
A pillar of strength to the state?
What for my girl? That she should be
The friend of the poor and desolate?

I do not ask they shall never tread
With weary feet the paths of pain.
I ask that in the darkest hour
They may faithful and true remain.

I only ask their lives may be
Pure as gems in the gates of pearl,
Lives to brighten and bless the world –
This I ask for my boy and girl.

I ask to clasp their hands again
'Mid the holy hosts of heaven,
Enraptured say: 'I am here, oh! God,
'And the children Thou hast given.'

Frances Ellen Watkins (1825–1911)

To My First Born

Fair tiny rosebud! What a tide
   Of hidden joy, o'erpow'ring, deep,
Of grateful love, of woman's pride,
   Thrills through my heart till I must weep
With bliss to look on thee, my son,
My first born child, my darling one!

What joy for me to sit and gaze
   Upon thy gentle, baby face,
And, dreaming of far distant days,
   With mother's weakness strive to trace
Tokens of future greatness high,
On thy smooth brow and lustrous eye.

What do I wish thee, darling, say?
   Is it that lordly mental power
That o'er thy kind will give thee sway,
   Unchanging, full, a glorious dower
For those whose minds may grasp its worth,
True rulers and true kings of earth?

Or would I ask for thee that fire
   Of wond'rous genius, great divine,
The spell that charms the poet's lyre,
   Till like a halo it will shine
Around a name praised, honored, sung,
In distant climes by many a tongue?

Ah, no! My child, with such vain themes
   I will not mar thy quiet rest
Nor wish ambition's restless dreams
   Infused into thy tranquil breast;
Too soon will manhood's weight of care
O'ercloud that waxen brow so fair.

For thee, my Babe, I only pray
   Thou'lt live to bless thy parents' love,
To be their hope, their earthly stay,
   And gaining grace from heaven above,
Tread in the path the good have trod,
True to thy country and thy God!

Rosanna Eleanor Leprohon (1829–79)

To a Young Girl With an Album

Gentle Lily with this Album my warmest wishes take,
I know its pages oft thou'lt ope and prize it for my sake,
For, though a trifling offering, it bears the magic spell
Of coming from the hand of one who loves thee passing well.

O could thy young life's course be traced by will or wish of mine,
A smiling, joyous future – a bright lot would be thine,
No cloud should mar the gladness of thy fair youth's
   op'ning morn,
The roses of thy girlhood should be free from blight or thorn.

Howe'er, 'tis better ordered by a Blessed Power above
Who sends us cross and trial, as a token of His Love;
For we'd cling, ah! Far too closely to earthly joys and ties,
Unwilling e'er to leave them for our home beyond the skies.

As the pages of this volume, unwritten, stainless, fair,
Life opens out before thee, let it be thine aim and care
To keep the record spotless, and ever free from all
That thou might'st wish hereafter remorseful to recall.

Not seeking to o'ershadow thy smiling azure eyes,
Nor see that girlish bosom heave with sad thoughts and sighs,
I would whisper low, while wishing thee, all earthly,
    cloudless bliss,
Be life a preparation for a better life than this!

Rosanna Eleanor Leprohon (1829–79)

E. Phillips Fox

The Mother Moon

The moon upon the wide sea
Placidly looks down,
Smiling with her mild face,
Though the ocean frown.
Clouds may dim her brightness,
But soon they pass away,
And she shines out, unaltered,
O'er the little waves at play.
So 'mid the storm or sunshine,
Wherever she may go,
Led on by her hidden power
The wild see must plow.

As the tranquil evening moon
Looks on that restless sea,
So a mother's gentle face,
Little child, is watching thee.
Then banish every tempest,
Chase all your clouds away,
That smoothly and brightly
Your quiet heart may play.
Let cheerful looks and actions
Like shining ripples flow,
Following the mother's voice,
Singing as they go.

Louisa May Alcott (1832–88)

Mother and Son

Postman, good postman, halt I pray,
And leave a letter for me to-day;
If it's only a line from over the sea
To say that my Sandy remembers me.

I have waited and hoped by day and by night;
I'll watch, if spared, till my locks grow white;
Have prayed, yet repent that my faith waxed dim,
When passing, you left no message from him.

My proud arms cradled his infant head,
My prayers arose by his boyhood's bed;
To better our fortunes, he traversed the main;
God guard him, and bring him to me again.

The postman has passed midst the beating rain,
And my heart is bowed with its weight of pain;
This dark, dark day, I am tortured with dread
That Sandy, my boy, may be ill or dead.

But hark! There's a step! My heart be still!
A step at the gate, in the path, on the sill;
Did the postman return? My letter forget?
Oh 'tis Sandy! Thank God, he loves me yet!

Mary Eliza Ireland (1834–1920)

Not a Child

I
'Not a child: I call myself a boy,'
Says my king, with accent stern yet mild,
Now nine years have brought him change of joy;
    'Not a child.'

How could reason be so far beguiled,
Err so far from sense's safe employ,
Stray so wide of truth, or run so wild?

Seeing his face bent over book or toy,
Child I called him, smiling: but he smiled
Back, as one too high for vain annoy –
    Not a child.

II
Not a child? Alack the year!
What should ail an undefiled
Heart, that he would fain appear
    Not a child?

Men, with years and memories piled
Each on other, far and near,
Fain again would so be styled:

Fain would cast off hope and fear,
Rest, forget, be reconciled:
Why would you so fain be, dear,
   Not a child?

III

Child or boy, my darling, which you will,
Still your praise finds heart and song employ,
Heart and song both yearning toward you still,
   Child or boy.

All joys else might sooner pall or cloy
Love than this which inly takes its fill,
Dear, of sight of your more perfect joy.

Nay, be aught you please, let all fulfil
All your pleasure; be your world your toy:
Mild or wild we love you, loud or still,
   Child or boy.

Algernon Charles Swinburne (1837–1909)

To My Daughter on Her Birthday

Darling child, to thee I owe,
More than others here will know;
Thou hast cheered my weary days,
With thy coy and winsome ways.
When my heart has been most sad,
Smile of thine has made me glad;
In return, I wish for thee,
Health and sweet felicity.
May thy future days be blest,
With all things the world deems best.
If perchance the day should come,
Thou does leave thy childhood's home;
Bound by earth's most sacred ties,
With responsibilities,
In another's life to share,
Wedded joys and worldly care;
May thy partner worthy prove
Richest in thy constant love.

Strong in faith and honour, just,
With brave heart on which to trust.
One, to whom when troubles come,
And the days grow burdensome,
Thou canst fly, with confidence
In his love's plenipotence.
And if when some years have flown,
Sons and daughters of your own
Bless your union, may they be
Wellsprings of pure joy to thee.
And when age shall line thy brow,
And thy step is weak and slow,
And the end of life draws near
May'st thou meet it without fear;
Undismayed with earth's alarms,
Sleeping, to wake in Jesus' arms.

John Hartley (1839–1917)

Baby's First Journey

Lightly they hold him and lightly they sway him –
Soft as a pillow are somebody's arms.
Down he goes slowly, ever so lowly
Over the rim of the cradle they lay him –
Baby's first journey is free from alarms.

Baby is growing while Mama sings by-lo,
Sturdy and rosy and laughing and fair,
Crowing and growing past every one's knowing,
Out goes the cradle and in comes the 'high-lo,'
Baby's next journey is into this chair.

Crying or cooing or waking or sleeping,
Baby is ever a thing to adore.
Look at him yonder – oh what a wonder,
Who would believe it, the darling is creeping,
Baby's next journey is over the floor.

Sweeter and cuter and brighter and stronger,
Mama can see every day how he's grown.
Shoes are all battered, stockings all tattered,
Oh! But the baby is baby no longer
Look at the fellow – he's walking alone!

Ella Wheeler Wilcox (1850–1919)

The First Step

My little one begins his feet to try,
A tottering, feeble, inconsistent way;
Pleased with the effort, he forgets his play,
And leaves his infant baubles where they lie.
Laughing and proud his mother flutters nigh,
Turning to go, yet joy-compelled to stay,
And, bird-like, singing what her heart would say;
But not so certain of my bliss am I.
For I bethink me of the days in store
Wherein those feet must traverse realms unknown,
And half forget the pathway to our door.
And I recall that in the seasons flown
We were his all – as he was all our own –
But never can be quite so any more.

Andrew Bice Saxton (b.1856)

Mother to Child

How best can I serve thee, my child! My child!
Flesh of my flesh and dear heart of my heart!
Once thou wast within me – I held thee – I fed thee –
By the force of my loving and longing I led thee –
    Now we are apart!

I may blind thee with kisses and crush with embracing,
Thy warm mouth in my neck and our arms interlacing;
But here in my body my soul lives alone,
And thou answerest me from a house of thine own –
    The house which I builded!

Which we builded together, thy father and I;
In which thou must live, O my darling, and die!
Not one stone can I alter, one atom relay –
Not to save or defend thee or help thee to stay –
    That gift is completed!

How best can I serve thee? O child, if they knew
How my heart aches with loving! How deep and how true,
How brave and enduring, how patient, how strong,
How longing for good and how fearful of wrong,
    Is the love of thy mother!

Could I crown thee with riches! Surround, overflow thee
With fame and with power till the whole world should know thee;
With wisdom and genius to hold the world still,
To bring laughter and tears, joy and pain, at thy will,
    Still – thou mightst not be happy!

Such have lived – and in sorrow. The greater the mind
The wider and deeper the grief it can find.
The richer, the gladder, the more thou canst feel
The keen stings that a lifetime is sure to reveal.
    O my child! Must thou suffer?

Is there no way my life can save thine from a pain?
Is the love of a mother no possible gain?
No labor of Hercules – search for the Grail –
No way for this wonderful love to avail?
    God in Heaven – O teach me!

My prayer has been answered. The pain thou must bear
Is the pain of the world's life which thy life must share,
Thou art one with the world – though I love thee the best;
And to save thee from pain I must save all the rest –
    Well – with God's help I'll do it.

Thou art one with the rest. I must love thee in them.
Thou wilt sin with the rest; and thy mother must stem
The world's sin. Thou wilt weep, and thy mother must dry
The tears of the world lest her darling should cry.
    I will do it – God helping!

And I stand not alone. I will gather a band
Of all loving mothers from land unto land.
Our children are part of the world! Do ye hear?
They are one with the world – we must hold them
    all dear!
    Love all for the child's sake!

For the sake of my child I must hasten to save
All the children on earth from the jail and the grave.
For so, and so only, I lighten the share
Of the pain of the world that my darling must bear –
    Even so, and so only!

Charlotte Perkins S. Gilman (1860–1935)

The Wish

That you might happier be than all the rest,
Than I who have been happy loving you,
Of all the innocent even the happiest –
This I beseeched for you.

Until I thought of those unending skies,
Of stagnant cloud, or fleckless dull blue air,
Of days and nights delightless, no surprise,
No threat, no sting, no fear;

And of the stirless waters of the mind,
Waveless, unfurrowed, of no living hue,
With dead eaves dropping slowly in no wind,
And nothing flowering new.

And then no more I wished you happiness,
But that whatever fell of joy or woe
I would not dare, O Sweet, to wish it less,
Or wish you less than you.

John Freeman (1880–1929)

A Joyful Song of Five

Come, let us all sing very high
And all sing very loud
And keep on singing in the street
Until there's quite a crowd;

And keep on singing in the house
And up and down the stairs;
Then underneath the furniture
Let's all play Polar bears;

And crawl about with doormats on,
And growl and howl and squeak,
Then in the garden let us fly
And play at hide and seek;

And 'Here we gather Nuts and May,'
'I wrote a Letter' too,
'Here we go round the Mulberry Bush,'
'The Child who lost its shoe';

And every game we ever played.
And then – to stay alive –
Let's end with lots of Birthday Cake
Because to-day you're five.

Katherine Mansfield (1888–1923)

On a Young Lady's Sixth Anniversary

Baby Babbles – only one,
Now to sit up has begun.

Little Babbles quite turned two
Walks as well as I and you.

And Miss Babbles one, two, three,
Has a teaspoon at her tea.

But her Highness at four
Learns to open the front door.

And her Majesty – now six,
Can her shoestrings neatly fix.

Babbles, babbles, have a care,
You will soon put up your hair!

Katherine Mansfield (1888–1923)

When Even Cometh On

The mother-heart doth yearn at eventide,
And, wheresoe'er the straying ones may roam,
When even cometh on they all fare home.
'Neath feathered sheltering the brood doth hide;
In eager flights the birds wing to their nest,
While happy lambs and children miss the sun,
And to the folds do hurtle one by one,
As night doth gather slowly in the west.
All ye who hurry through life's busy day,
Hark to the greeting that the Ages tell,
'The sun doth rise and set, hail and farewell.'
But comfort ye your heart where'er ye stray,
For those who through this little day do roam,
When even cometh on shall all fare home.

Lucy Evangeline Tilley (19th century)

ODE TO MOTHERS

To My Mother

They tell us of an Indian tree,
    Which, howsoe'er the sun and sky
May tempt its boughs to wander free,
    And shoot and blossom wide and high,
Far better loves to bend its arms
    Downward again to that dear earth,
From which the life that, fills and warms
    Its grateful being, first had birth.
'Tis thus, tho' wooed by flattering friends,
    And fed with fame (if fame it be)
This heart, my own dear mother, bends,
    With love's true instinct, back to thee!

Thomas Moore (1779–1852)

Sonnet, For My Mother's Birthday

At thy approach, oh, sweet bewitching May!
Through ev'ry wood soft melodies resound;
On silken wings Favonian breezes play,
And scatter bloom and fragrance all around!

Yet not for these I hail thy gentle reign,
And rove enchanted through thy fairy bow'rs;
Not for thy warbled songs, thy zephyr-train,
Nor all the incense of thy glowing flow'rs.

For this to thee I pour the artless lay,
Oh, lovely May! Thou goddess of the grove!
With thee returns the smiling natal day,
Of her, who claims my fond, my filial love!
Bright as thy sun-beams may it still appear,
Calm as thy skies, unclouded with a tear!

Felicia Dorothea Hemans (1793–1835)

Extract from To My Mother

Because I feel that, in the Heavens above,
The angels, whispering to one another,
Can find, among their burning terms of love,
None so devotional as that of 'Mother,'
Therefore by that dear name I long have called you….

Edgar Allen Poe (1809–49)

My Blessed Mother

My blessed Mother dozing in her chair
On Christmas Day seem'd an embodied Love,
A comfortable Love with soft brown hair
Softened and silvered to a tint of dove;
A better sort of Venus with an air
Angelical from thoughts that dwell above;
A wiser Pallas in whose body fair
Enshrined a blessed soul looks out thereof.
Winter brought holly then;
Now spring has brought
Paler and frailer snowdrops shivering;
And I have brought a simple humble thought –
I her devoted duteous Valentine –
A lifelong thought which thrills this song I sing,
A lifelong love to this dear Saint of mine.

Christina Georgina Rossetti (1830–94)

Sonnets Are Full of Love

Sonnets are full of love, and this my tome
Has many sonnets: so here now shall be
One sonnet more, a love sonnet, from me
To her whose heart is my heart's quiet home,
To my first Love, my Mother, on whose knee
I learnt love-lore that is not troublesome;
Whose service is my special dignity,
And she my loadstar while I go and come
And so because you love me, and because
I love you, Mother, I have woven a wreath
Of rhymes wherewith to crown your honored name:
In you not fourscore years can dim the flame
Of love, whose blessed glow transcends the laws
Of time and change and mortal life and death.

Christina Georgina Rossetti (1830–94)

To My Mother

To-day's your natal day;
   Sweet flowers I bring:
Mother, accept, I pray
   My offering.

And may you happy live,
   And long us bless;
Receiving as you give
   Great happiness.

Christina Georgina Rossetti (1830–94)

Only One

Hundreds of stars in the pretty sky,
Hundreds of shells on the shore together,
Hundreds of birds that go singing by,
Hundreds of birds in the sunny weather.

Hundreds of dewdrops to greet the dawn,
Hundreds of bees in the purple clover,
Hundreds of butterflies on the lawn,
But only one mother the wide world over.

George Cooper (1840–1927)

My Infant Days

When I was a little infant,
    And I lay in mother's arms,
Then I felt the gentle pressure
    Of a loving mother's arms.
'Go to sleep my little baby,
    Go to sleep,' mamma would say;
'Oh, will not my little lady
    Go to sleep for ma to-day.'

Oh! My parents loved me dearly,
    For I was their eldest born,
And they always called me Julia
    In a mild and loving form.
My parents will not forget me,
    Though I married and left their home,
For they can remember clearly
    How with them I once did roam.

Oh! My mother, how I love her,
    Though her head is growing gray,
For in fancy I can see her
    Bending o'er me night and day,
As she did when I was little,
    Watching me in sleep and play –
Mother now is growing feeble,
    Now I will her love repay.

Oh! My father, how I love him,
    For he has worked hard for me,
For to earn my food and clothing,
    In my little infancy.
And oh, I will not forget him,
    While on earth I do remain –
May the God of heaven bless him
    In this world of grief and pain.

Julia A. Moore (1847–1920)

My Vision

Wherever my feet may wander
    Wherever I chance to be,
There comes, with the coming of even' time
    A vision sweet to me.
I see my mother sitting
    In the old familiar place,
And she rocks to the tune her needles sing,
    And thinks of an absent face.

I can hear the roar of the city
    About me now as I write;
But over an hundred miles of snow
    My thought-steeds fly tonight,
To the dear little cozy cottage,
    And the room where mother sits,
And slowly rocks in her easy chair
    And thinks of me as she knits.

Sometimes with the merry dancers
    When my feet are keeping time,
And my heart beats high, as young hearts will,
    To the music's rhythmic chime.
My spirit slips over the distance
    Over the glitter and whirl,
To my mother who sits, and rocks, and knits,
    And thinks of her 'little girl.'

And when I listen to voices that flatter,
    And smile, as women do,
To whispered words that may be sweet,
    But are not always true;
I think of the sweet, quaint picture
    Afar in quiet ways,
And I know one smile of my mother's eyes
    Is better than all their praise.

And I know I can never wander
    Far from the path of right,
Though snares are set for a woman's feet
    In places that seem most bright.
For the vision is with me always,
    Wherever I chance to be,
Of mother sitting, rocking, and knitting,
    Thinking and praying for me.

Ella Wheeler Wilcox (1850–1919)

A Prayer For a Mother's Birthday

Lord Jesus, Thou hast known
A mother's love and tender care:
And Thou wilt hear, while for my own
Mother most dear I make this birthday prayer.

Protect her life, I pray,
Who gave the gift of life to me;
And may she know, from day to day,
The deepening glow of Life that comes from Thee.

As once upon her breast
Fearless and well content I lay,
So let her heart, on Thee at rest,
Feel fears depart and troubles fade away.

Her every wish fulfill;
And even if Thou must refuse
In anything, let Thy wise will
A comfort bring such as kind mothers use.

Ah, hold her by the hand,
As once her hand held mine;
And though she may not understand
Life's winding way, lead her in peace divine.

I cannot pay my debt
For all the love that she has given;
But Thou, love's Lord, wilt not forget
Her due reward, bless her in earth and heaven.

Henry van Dyke (1852–1933)

Family Love

I adore my dear mother,
I adore my dear father too;
No one loves me as much
As they know how to love me.

When I sleep, they keep watch over me;
When I cry they are sad with me;
When I laugh they smile with me:
My laugh is the sunshine for them.

They tenderly teach me
To be happy and nice.
My father does his best for me;
My mother prays always for me.

I adore my dear mother,
I adore my dear father too.
No one loves me as much
As they know how to love me.

Amado Ruiz de Nervo (1870–1919)

Songs For My Mother

Her Hands

My mother's hands are cool and fair,
They can do anything.
Delicate mercies hide them there
Like flowers in the spring.

When I was small and could not sleep,
She used to come to me,
And with my cheek upon her hand
How sure my rest would be.

For everything she ever touched
Of beautiful or fine,
Their memories living in her hands
Would warm that sleep of mine.

Her hands remember how they played
One time in meadow streams,
And all the flickering song and shade
Of water took my dreams.

Swift through her haunted fingers pass
Memories of garden things;
I dipped my face in flowers and grass
And sounds of hidden wings.

One time she touched the cloud that kissed
Brown pastures bleak and far;
I leaned my cheek into a mist
And thought I was a star.

All this was very long ago
And I am grown; but yet
The hand that lured my slumber so
I never can forget.

For still when drowsiness comes on
It seems so soft and cool,
Shaped happily beneath my cheek,
Hollow and beautiful.

Her Words

My mother has the prettiest tricks
Of words and words and words.
Her talk comes out as smooth and sleek
As breasts of singing birds.

She shapes her speech all silver fine
Because she loves it so.
And her own eyes begin to shine
To hear her stories grow.

And if she goes to make a call
Or out to take a walk
We leave our work when she returns
And run to hear her talk.

We had not dreamed these things were so
Of sorrow and of mirth.
Her speech is as a thousand eyes
Through which we see the earth.

God wove a web of loveliness,
Of clouds and stars and birds,
But made not any thing at all
So beautiful as words.

They shine around our simple earth
With golden shadowings,
And every common thing they touch
Is exquisite with wings.

There's nothing poor and nothing small
But is made fair with them.
They are the hands of living faith
That touch the garment's hem.

They are as fair as bloom or air,
They shine like any star,
And I am rich who learned from her
How beautiful they are.

Anna Hempstead Branch (1875–1937)

To My Mother

No foreign tribute from a stranger-hand,
Mother, I bring thee, whom not Heaven's songs
Would as an alien reach.... Ah, but how far
From Heaven's least heavenly is the changing note
And changing fancy of these fitful cries!
Mother, forgive them, as the best of me
Has ever pleaded only for thy pardon,
Not for thy praise. Mother, there is a love
Men give to wives and children, lovers, friends;
There is a love which some men give to God.
Ah! Between this, I think, and that last love,
Last and too-late-discovered love of God,
There shines – and nearer to the love of God –
The love a man gives only to his mother,
Whose travail of dear thought has never end
Until the End. Oh that my mouth had words
Comfortable as thy kisses to the boy
Who loved while he forgot thee! Now I love,
Sundered and far, with daily heart's remembrance
The face the wind brings to me, the sun lights,
The birds and waters sing; the face of thee
Whom I love with a love like love of God.

John Freeman (1880–1929)

My Mother

God made my mother on an April day,
From sorrow and the mist along the sea,
Lost birds' and wanderers' songs and ocean spray,
And the moon loved her wandering jealously.

Beside the ocean's din she combed her hair,
Singing the nocturne of the passing ships,
Before her earthly lover found her there
And kissed away the music from her lips.

She came unto the hills and saw the change
That brings the swallow and the geese in turns.
But there was not a grief she deeméd strange,
For there is that in her which always mourns.

Kind heart she has for all on hill or wave
Whose hopes grew wings like ants to fly away.
I bless the God Who such a mother gave
This poor bird-hearted singer of a day.

Francis Ledwidge (1887–1917)

Picture Credits

5 Courtesy of Foundry Arts

5 Courtesy of Foundry Arts

9 Theodore Gerard (1829–95) The Newborn Child. Courtesy of Private Collection/The Bridgeman Art Library

0 Courtesy of Foundry Arts

5 Hamilton Hamilton (1847–1928) Falling Apple Blossoms. Courtesy of Private Collection, Phillips, Fine Art Auctioneers, New York, USA/The Bridgeman Art Library

7 Thomas Webster (1800–86) Sickness and Health, 1843. Courtesy of Victoria & Albert Museum, London, UK/The Bridgeman Art Library

8 Pierre Auguste Renoir (1841–1919) Gabrielle and Jean, c.1895–56. Courtesy of Musee de l'Orangerie, Paris, France, Lauros/Giraudon/The Bridgeman Art Library

1, 122 Fritz von Uhde (1848–1911) The Nursery, 1889. Courtesy of Hamburger Kunsthalle, Hamburg, Germany/The Bridgeman Art Library

4 Courtesy of Foundry Arts

8 Courtesy of Foundry Arts

4 Courtesy of Foundry Arts

2–53 Philip Richard Morris (1838–1902) The First Born, c.1875. © Harris Museum and Art Gallery, Preston, Lancashire, UK/The Bridgeman Art Library

7 Courtesy of Foundry Arts

8 Henri Gervex (1852–1929) Colette's First Steps, 1895. Courtesy of Private Collection, Giraudon/The Bridgeman Art Library

1 Charles Lucy (1814–73) Sunny Hours. Courtesy of Private Collection, © Agnew's, London, UK/The Bridgeman Art Library

5 Courtesy of Foundry Arts

6 Mary Stevenson Cassatt (1844–1926) The Young Mother. Courtesy of Private Collection, Photo © Christie's Images/The Bridgeman Art Library

8–49 Boris Mihajlovic Kustodiev (1878–1927) Morning, 1910. Courtesy of State Russian Museum, St. Petersburg, Russia/The Bridgeman Art Library

0 George Goodwin Kilburne (1839–1924) Mother's Little Helper. Courtesy of Private Collection, © Mallett Gallery, London, UK/The Bridgeman Art Library

3 Courtesy of Foundry Arts

54 Joseph Clark (1834–1926) Good Bye Baby. Courtesy of Private Collection/The Bridgeman Art Library

9 Gustave Leonard de Jonghe (1829–93) Motherly Love. Courtesy of Berko Fine Paintings, Knokke-Zoute, Belgium/The Bridgeman Art Library

160 Mary Stevenson Cassatt (1844–1926) Mother Combing Her Child's Hair, c.1901. Courtesy of Brooklyn Museum of Art, New York, USA, Bequest of Mary T. Cockcroft/The Bridgeman Art Library

162–63 Victor Gabriel Gilbert (1847–1933) Playing with the Hoop. Courtesy of Josef Mensing Gallery, Hamm-Rhynern, Germany/The BridgemanArt Library

164, 165 Charles West Cope (1811–90) Convalescent. Courtesy of Private Collection, © Mallett Gallery, London, UK/The Bridgeman Art Library

170 Jules Ernest Renoux (1863–1932) Weaning. Courtesy of Private Collection, © DACS/Giraudon/The Bridgeman Art Library

173 Courtesy of Foundry Arts

175 Courtesy of Foundry Arts

176 Berthe Morisot (1841–95) Child in the Hollyhocks, 1881. Courtesy of Private Collection, Photo © Christie's Images/The Bridgeman Art Library

179 Courtesy of Foundry Arts

181 Edouard Manet (1832–83) Washerwoman, 1875. © The Barnes Foundation, Merion, Pennsylvania, USA/The Bridgeman Art Library

182 Lionel Percy Smythe (1839–1918) The Arabian Nights, 1865. Courtesy of Private Collection/The Bridgeman Art Library

185 Courtesy of Foundry Arts

186 Frederick James McNamara Evans (fl.1886–1930) A Fair Crop. © The Trehayes Collection, Cornwall, UK/The Bridgeman Art Library

189 Courtesy of Foundry Arts

190 Henri Jules Jean Geoffroy (1853–1924) The Drop of Milk in Belleville: Doctor Variot's Surgery, The Weighing Session, 1903. Courtesy of Musee de l'Assistance Publique, Hopitaux de Paris, France, Giraudon/The Bridgeman Art Library

195 James Hayllar (1829–1920) Miss Lily's Return from the Ball, 1866. Courtesy of Private Collection, © Mallett Gallery, London, UK/The Bridgeman Art Library

199 Charles West Cope (1811–90) Breakfast Time – Morning Games. Courtesy of Private Collection, Photo © Bonhams, London, UK/The Bridgeman Art Library

200 Courtesy of Foundry Arts

203 Courtesy of Foundry Arts

205 Courtesy of Foundry Arts

Index of Titles

Index of Poets